ISBN:

978-1-7339445-0-2

ILLUSTRATIONS BY:

IRINA PAMYANTNIH

LAYOUT DESIGN BY:

ROSEN TODOROVSKY

PHOTOGRAPHY BY:

LAIBEL SCHWARTZ

OTHER CONTRIBUTORS:

CYNTHIA GEIGEL

BEVERLEY GREENBERG

JUDITH GREENBERG

ISAAC PONTE

SHELDON SOPER

THE BIG BOOK OF
ECOMMERCE INSIGHTS

JEREMY ISAAC GREENBERG

CONTENTS

WHY YOU SHOULD TRANSFORM YOUR THIRD-PARTY SALES INTO A FIRST-PARTY BUSINESS 9

SELLING USED PRODUCTS DOESN'T MAKE YOU A SNAKE OIL SALESMAN 17

IS AMAZON PRIME FINALLY LOSING ITS FOOTHOLD? 27

IS THE GOVERNMENT GOING TO BREAK UP AMAZON.COM? 35

HOW THE END OF AN INTERNATIONAL SHIPPING TREATY WILL HELP U.S. SELLERS 43

HOW AMAZON'S NEW BRAND STRATEGY IMPACTS PRIVATE LABEL SELLERS 53

IS YOUR BUSINESS PREPARED FOR AMAZON'S PAY BY INVOICE SERVICE? 63

WHAT DOES A US-CHINA TRADE WAR MEAN FOR YOUR ECOMMERCE BUSINESS? 69

HOW THE SUPREME COURT'S SALES TAX DECISION WILL IMPACT YOUR ECOMMERCE BUSINESS 77

PROPOSITION 65 AND HOW TO PROTECT YOUR BUSINESS FROM COMPLIANCE VIOLATIONS 87

WHAT AMAZON'S "AUTO-AUTHORIZED RETURNS" POLICY MEANS FOR YOUR BUSINESS 95

DEATH OF THE DAILY DEAL 105

HOW TO MAINTAIN PROFITABILITY DESPITE USPS RATE HIKES 115

HOW TO LEVERAGE FOREIGN CURRENCY VOLATILITY IN YOUR ECOMMERCE BUSINESS 121

A MESSAGE TO YOU

I started SellerCloud over a decade ago to address challenges faced by local sellers. One thing that I learned early on is that a great system cannot be modeled after a single client. Each of my clients has taught me valuable lessons that have enhanced my understanding of ecommerce and provided insight into the needs of the marketplace as a whole.

My ongoing interactions with the SellerCloud community have put me in a unique position from which I can see the big picture more clearly. This vision results in a platform that is more robust, versatile and able to better meet your needs. The constant feedback that you provide continues to fuel innovation at SellerCloud and refinement of our feature set.

In this book I've included some of our recently written articles that focus on ecommerce topics and how they relate to our client base. I hope that in reading these articles you can gain some new ideas about the industry as well as an appreciation for the effort that we make everyday to keep SellerCloud ahead of the curve.

**JEREMY ISAAC GREENBERG,
FOUNDER & CEO**

WHY YOU SHOULD TRANSFORM YOUR THIRD-PARTY SALES INTO A FIRST-PARTY BUSINESS

People often ask me, "Where are biggest third-party marketplaces after Amazon?" The answer isn't always what they are expecting.

With Amazon continuing to grow as an international retail powerhouse, third-party sellers are finding it increasingly more challenging to achieve the same financial successes they could once rely on. The more sellers enter the marketplace, the fewer sales and profits there are to go around. It makes sense that sellers are increasingly searching for greener pastures.

However, what sellers should really be asking is, "What is the next biggest opportunity for sales beyond Amazon?", not "where".

The answer is first-party sales.

The difference between first-party and third-party sales

Third-party ecommerce businesses market and sell products directly to consumers through a channel like Amazon or eBay. Sellers pay a fee for the privilege – typically on a per sale basis.

In a first-party relationship, sellers become wholesalers. They sell their inventory to retailers like Amazon, Walmart, or Wayfair who then sell the products in their own retail marketplaces. These larger retailers set the prices and market the products as their own inventory.

There has been loud criticism of the wholesale model as an antiquated and dying form of retail. With the transition from brick-and-mortar stores to ecommerce and decentralized distribution, images of aisles and warehouses of retail goods seem poised to become the relics of a bygone age.

While that argument might make sense on paper, what people don't realize is that conventional first-party business concepts (including wholesale) are actually gaining traction with both online sellers and larger retailers.

In a first-party arrangement, sellers can take advantage of more efficient and cost-effective distribution channels than third-party sellers can. At the same time, first-party vendors allow retailers to increase the variety of products available on their websites and in their stores so that they are better equipped to serve visitors' purchasing demands.

In a first-party relationship, sellers become wholesalers

As a result, selling as a first-party can often wind up becoming more reliable and profitable for an ecommerce business than selling as a third-party.

Why moving to first-party sales makes sense
- Higher margins

Retail marketplaces like Amazon and Walmart have become increasingly crowded with sellers of similar merchandise undercutting each other's prices. This means sellers of the most popular products are often forced to sell at paper-thin margins to compete for customers. As such, sellers must sell at larger and larger volumes just to ensure a profit.

In contrast, it is possible as a first-party business to reduce the extra costs associated with third-party sales while also increasing margins and remaining competitive in the same online marketplaces.

- Diversified businesses carry lower risks

In most cases, businesses put themselves at risk when they rely on a single customer for more than 15% of their sales. For many ecommerce businesses, Amazon sales far surpass that threshold.

One problem with this is that Amazon's policy shifts tend to make selling on their platform increasingly beneficial for buyers at the expense of sellers. With most third-party sellers already operating on slim margins, all it takes is a single change to the terms of service to make a once-profitable arrangement potentially unsustainable.

Transitioning from third-party to first-party sales is a great way to both diversify your potential customer base while also mitigating the risks associated with an overreliance on a single retail channel like Amazon.

- Building a brand can lead to business growth

Many third-party sellers are effectively glorified middlemen. Customers seek out products on digital retail platforms and third-party sellers scramble and

Many third-party sellers are effectively glorified middlemen

claw over each other to see who can fill the demand the most cheaply and efficiently.

In this model, the purchasers typically don't care about the seller or the seller's business – third parties are viewed as little more than nameless, faceless fulfillment resources on a per-sale basis.

In contrast, first-party sellers are much more than a means to some other company's profitable ends. By assuming the role of the wholesaler, first-party sellers gain the ability to supply their own branded, private label products to the marketplace in much the same way that a traditional manufacturer would.

The script is flipped and the retailers become the middlemen. The large retailer, not the seller, is tasked with doing the work of marketing the seller's branded products to consumers.

Meanwhile, each sale becomes an opportunity for the first-party business to both establish an identity and connect with clients as a company.

Savvy first-party sellers can lean on their unique merchandise and/or unique wholesale relationships to sidestep the ruthless third-party competition for the most popular products while also bolstering their own brand awareness.

First-party dropshipping is a viable pathway to growth

Transitioning from third-party to first-party sales may seem daunting. It used to be that becoming a wholesale vendor to a major retailer was a difficult and expensive proposition. Niche sellers faced seemingly insurmountable odds in pursuit of shelf space or website visibility.

Not anymore.

Dropshipping has made it possible for ecommerce sellers of all sizes to serve as first-party vendors to some of the largest retailers on the planet. What's more, the infrastructure to make this transition is already in place.

Simply put, dropshipping is a way for retailers to sell products to customers without ever having to hold the products as inven-

First-party sellers are much more than a means to some other company's profitable ends

tory. Instead, when a product is sold, the retailer buys it from a supplier and has it sent directly to the purchaser.

Successful internet sellers are in the perfect position to serve as dropship suppliers. The same reliable shipping infrastructure required to thrive as a profitable third-party seller is what major retailers look for in building their dropshipping networks.

For years, SellerCloud has been managing these types of Electronic Data Interchange (EDI) integrations on behalf of our customers. Back in 2012 it began helping customers serve as dropship suppliers for Wayfair and Overstock and soon after expanded to include retailers like Target, Home Depot, and Kohls.

Historically, establishing EDI channels has been an expensive proposition. Smaller sellers in particular are priced out by long contracts, fees for enabling channels, and steep costs per file transmission or per kilo-character.

SellerCloud's direct integration agreements with the aforementioned companies, and now with Amazon Vendor Central and Walmart DSV (Dropship Vendor), simplify the process for ecommerce retailers of all sizes. With SellerCloud, there are no extra EDI or value-added network (VAN) related fees to extend business into these strong sales channels. Instead, there is just a simple per-order fee – just like any other marketplace order.

Becoming a first-party seller is also a viable option for ecommerce businesses looking to diversify and strengthen their market presence beyond the online space. Several national retail chains like JCPenny and Sears's have begun using their online dropship programs to vet new vendors for their stores. This means that businesses that establish themselves as reliable dropshipping suppliers for clients like these can see their products not only featured on popular websites but also featured on shelves in thousands of brick-and-mortar locations.

The first-party sales model is very much alive and well for those who know how to take advantage of it. Is your online retail business ready to make the leap from third-party to first-party? Contact SellerCloud directly to see how our platform can make the transition both painless and profitable.

Successful internet sellers are in the perfect position to serve as dropship suppliers

SELLING USED PRODUCTS DOESN'T MAKE YOU A SNAKE OIL SALESMAN

For many ecommerce retailers, the thought of selling used products seems like an act of desperation. Often, selling used goods is seen as a reputation killer that reduces a business into the same category as a slimy used car salesman or a turn-of-the-century grifter selling exotic potions out of a wagon – a business that is willing to go to an extreme to make a buck.

This is enough to keep most sellers out of the used merchandise space altogether. You can see the logic: Why sell opened, previously owned merchandise when you can sell brand-new, factory-sealed, products? Why take the risk of allowing negative reviews from used product transactions to affect your sales of new products?

While selling used goods certainly comes with challenges, it represents a new reality in what it takes to grow your ecommerce business. As online marketplaces continually make it easier for customers to return products to sellers (with or without cause), sellers are faced with a swelling pile of returned inventory that has value, but can no longer be sold as new. Often, this inventory is never resold at all.

Thankfully, there are still ways to transform that inventory from a loss into a profit. What's more, the SellerCloud inventory management system can help.

This isn't Rumpelstiltskin trying to spin straw into gold or the eccentric alchemist trying to magically transform lead bars. This is smart business.

Eliminate the unsellable inventory pile
Take a look at your inventory data. If you are like most ecommerce retailers, you are seeing higher percentages of returned sales than you did in past years. A large contributor to this trend is the growing empowerment and entitlement of the average online customer.

Everyone from Amazon to eBay, Walmart to Newegg has added simplified return policies that enable customers to easily return items to sellers for refunds – and customers are taking advantage. In the long term, these policies boost consumer confidence and convenience; they continue to steer more buyers toward online retail and away from brick-and-mortar stores. In the short term, these policies cause plenty of headaches for online sellers.

One of the major problems with this type of consumer behavior is that sellers are left to fig-

For many ecommerce retailers, the thought of selling used products seems like an act of desperation

ure out what to do with increasing quantities of returned inventory. Even if these products are in perfect condition, this merchandise can no longer be advertised and sold as new according to most state and federal laws as well as most online marketplace policies.

Once upon a time, sales were final and returns were prohibitively difficult for consumers. That fairy tale is over. Even eBay, known for making it easy to sell used goods, now requires every item on its platform to have a standard return option. Nowadays, you must be prepared that any items you sell might find their way back to you. Once they do, there is no magic wand that will transform those returned products into factory-sealed, brand-new inventory.

That leaves two options: discard what is likely perfectly good merchandise and eat the loss, or sell the inventory as used products at a discount and salvage a profit. Neither is ideal, but most business people would probably agree that the latter clearly outweighs the former.

If you are serious about maximizing your retail profits in today's ecommerce environment, you need a plan for reselling returned inventory. That means developing a system to bring returned merchandise up to the standards of today's picky consumers and strict marketplaces.

SellerCloud can help. Our tools enable sellers to navigate the return merchandise authorization (RMA) processes of the leading online marketplaces, account for returned inventory, and track products as they go through the necessary steps to become reconditioned and refurbished for sale. The process starts with an RMA shipping label. SellerCloud makes it easy to turn a customer's return into a seamless part of your inventory flow that is both trackable and reliable. As an added protection against loss, these RMA claims can issue return shipping labels to customers that are pay-on-use. This ensures that you are not charged for return shipping costs unless the label you send to the customer is actually scanned by the shipping company.

Once the returned package arrives back at the warehouse, the label's RMA barcode can be scanned in order to signal to warehouse employees that the item needs to be placed in quarantine where it will not mistakenly wind up back in the sellable inventory channel. This gives the seller an opportunity to inspect the inventory before deciding how to process the product for eventual resale.

Nowadays, you must be prepared that any items you sell might find their way back to you

Similarly, returns from Fulfillment by Amazon (FBA) orders can be 'removed' from the Amazon warehouse and be easily transitioned back into inventory if they are in perfect condition. However, this step relies on Amazon's warehouse staff to make the judgement call on the state of each returned item. If there is any question as to an item's quality, you can expect Amazon to err on the side of caution and flag an item as not sellable when, in fact, you might deem it worthy of being placed back into your available inventory.

Alternatively, SellerCloud also allows sellers to create credit memos for sending a returned product back to the manufacturer or vendor for a refund. Sellers can use serial number tracking features to trace the returned item back to the original purchase order and identify the appropriate vendor to contact.

Take advantage of marketplace certified refurbished programs

"Used" sounds like a dirty word. Label something as used and it conjures up the notion that it is unclean or has long since outlived its optimal usefulness. If given the choice of a new car or a used car, which would you opt for? What if instead of a car it was a pillow?

How about earbuds?

See what I mean?

Fortunately, most retailers have adopted language that helps sellers circumvent the negative connotation of the word used when it comes to marketing their "like-new" inventory.

Every ecommerce marketplace has its own terminology for high-quality used merchandise. Amazon offers Amazon Renewed products. Walmart features Certified Refurbished Electronics. eBay dedicates an entire webpage to Certified Pre-Owned items.

Whatever the marketing jargon of choice may be, these programs all essentially serve the same purpose: they scrutinize used merchandise with a set of standards designed to promote customer confidence. As a result, items given the title of "renewed," "refreshed," or "certified pre-owned" are expected to perform like their new counterparts. The products and their accessories are all accounted for and either in new or like-new condition.

Ultimately, these programs make it easier to transform returned items into sellable,

Ultimately, these programs make it easier to transform returned items into sellable, profitable inventory

profitable inventory.

For products that have received more use than just an opened package, there are refurbishing options that can bring the item into compliance with the rigorous standards of certified refurbished programs:

- Manufacturer refurbished products are repaired, cleaned, and inspected by either the manufacturer or one of its vendors to ensure that they are in perfect working condition. These products are often sold with warranty policies that are either identical or very similar to a new item.

- Seller refurbished products are repaired, cleaned, and inspected by someone other than the manufacturer or one of its vendors. The seller attests that each product has been repaired, cleaned, and inspected to ensure that it is in perfect, working condition. The seller may offer a warranty to further bolster consumer confidence.

- Ecommerce sites often mandate additional guarantees for refurbished products to signify faith that the products will hold up to consumer scrutiny. For instance, Walmart and Amazon each require a minimum 90-day seller-backed warranty for these types of "renewed" items.

Refurbishing has become particularly popular in the consumer electronics market. Customers can get their hands on expensive devices like smartphones, televisions, gaming systems, tablets, and PCs at steep discounts if they are willing to settle for refurbished instead of brand new. In many cases the only things separating these items from their brand-new counterparts are minor cosmetic nicks or broken warranty seals.

One of the leaders in this arena is Back Market, the largest reseller of refurbished products in Europe and a fast-growing newcomer in the American consumer space. Back Market's business model centers on reducing e-waste (6,300,000 tons of which was produced in 2018 in the U.S. alone) by refurbishing and reselling used consumer electronics at affordable prices and with a generous 6-month warranty. SellerCloud has recently integrated with Back Market due to the growing interest from our clients.

Ecommerce sites often mandate additional guarantees for refurbished products

Protect your brand by keeping your new and refurbished sales separate.

One of the main excuses sellers lean on to justify leaving returned inventory to sit unsold is the fear of negative feedback. After all, customers who were dissatisfied (for whatever reason) already returned the items once. Why risk it happening again?

It's true. There is naturally a higher rate of complaints for used and refurbished items. Similarly, negative feedback jeopardizes your selling power as a third-party retailer online. Amazon, for one, has a notoriously low tolerance for third-party sellers that accumulate even modest volumes of customer complaints.

As such, there is an obvious risk associated with marketing products to buyers whose expectations might be out of line with the reality of what they are purchasing. There are plenty of shoppers that will presume they are receiving perfectly new products regardless of how clear your descriptions of any imperfections may be. Making matters worse, most marketplaces will allow the disappointed customer to return the item and leave negative feedback regardless of wheth-

er he or she is in the right or not.

Chin up. Selling refurbished items is and will increasingly become an essential piece of successful online ecommerce. Getting in on the game now may be challenging and frustrating at times, but it is a necessary step. That said, you should be proactive in how you handle the used product portion of your business so that you are prepared for the occasional prickly buyers and be confident they won't tarnish your established reputation.

The important thing to remember is that just because your business sells refurbished items, this doesn't make it a used product business. The ability to transform unsellable inventory into profitable sales is what will mitigate losses and allow your sales of new products to thrive.

Before listing a single refurbished item, investigate the terms and options available to you on your preferred ecommerce marketplaces. The ideal option is to create multiple seller accounts on these platforms – keeping your new inventory on one account and marketing your refurbished inventory on another.

Selling refurbished items is and will increasingly become an essential piece of successful online ecommerce

Some sites like eBay allow one seller to have multiple eBay stores that are associated with each other. Other marketplaces, like Amazon, generally don't allow having multiple accounts but we have seen them allow it in circumstances like this, with special permission. Whether it is easier or more difficult, putting in the legwork up front to delineate between your new and used inventory will pay off in the end.

One important thing to bear in mind is to never list the same item with the same condition on both selling profiles. SellerCloud has the ability to configure inventory rules, what we call a custom inventory calculation, to help make sure that you are compliant with these types of requirements.

Once your accounts are established, SellerCloud can handle the process from there. Our inventory management system is equipped to handle multiple seller profiles within the same marketplace. SellerCloud also has the ability to flag your inventory designated for refurbished sales programs so that it can be processed differently than your orders for new products.

Combine those features with a reliable

RMA tracking system, integration with an ever-growing number of ecommerce marketplaces and services, and reliable customer support and you have a dependable partner that is ready to maximize the profitability of your entire inventory – new, refurbished, refreshed, or renewed.

Selling refurbished inventory may not be a fairy tale, but it doesn't have to make you the snake oil salesman performing in the town square, either. Schedule a live demo to see how SellerCloud can help you establish and manage your own reputable position in the used products space.

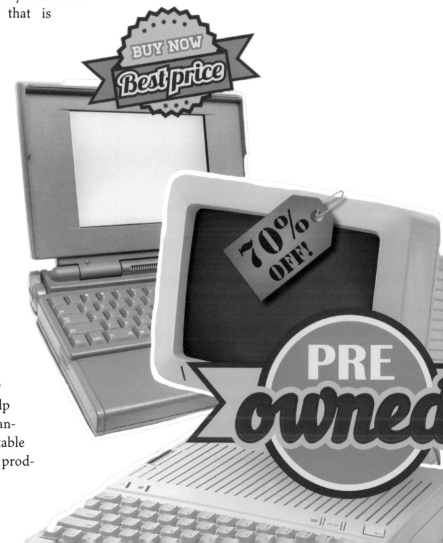

IS AMAZON PRIME FINALLY LOSING ITS FOOTHOLD?

With 5-billion packages shipped and some 310-million active customers worldwide, Amazon generated a whopping $177.9-billion in revenue just last year. As a whole, the company has a market value that hovers around $427-billion, and to put that in comparison, Walmart, which trails in second in the United States, is worth nearly half that at $221-billion.

To say that Amazon is a giant is an understatement. But, just because the online retailer created a phenomenon with 'Prime' that quickly obtained cult status doesn't mean they can't be overtaken by the pack of brick-and-mortar stores catching up. In fact, amidst rising competition on the digital frontier, Amazon is starting to leverage their own new, more integrated, and physical presence of Prime in its customer's lives to keep the lead. Let us explain.

What's changed?

Essentially, the competition caught up. After launching in 2005 and quickly soaring to popularity in the mid-2000's, the online retailer was synonymous with warehousing — offering low prices offset by purchasing popular products in bulk and selling them out of their own distribution centers. With Prime, consumers only had to click a few buttons to get items delivered for free within a couple of days — the convenience alone was revolutionary. Today, not as much.

While Amazon quickly captured much of the online retail market, brick and mortar stores were initially blindsided but then spent years trying to catch up. In the meantime, Amazon Prime forever changed how consumers expect the digital customer experience to be — seamless, convenient and including free shipping. Brick-and-mortar stores had to revamp their digital marketplaces and offer free shipping (often, on qualified items or after matching a certain pay threshold). Notably, they're also doing this without charging customers a yearly membership fee.

The competition also expanded and began offering perks to compete. eBay, for example, introduced its eBay Guaranteed Delivery program so that buyers can filter search results to show only those items that will arrive fast. Even if a seller has inventory in multiple warehouses they can offer a door-to-door guarantee on eBay using regional rate tables in SellerCloud. Similarly, Walmart now offers free 2-Day shipping on many products.

To say that Amazon is a giant is an understatement

Walmart has not only increased its focus on their digital retail space, but acquired various ecommerce companies like Jet.com, Shoebuy, and even Bare Necessities and continued to leverage its more than 6,000 brick-and-mortar stores to its advantage (i.e. order online and pick up in store).

So now that Prime isn't new, what's next?
Instead of trying to reinvent the wheel, Amazon is simply adding consumer-friendly perks that directly integrate the brand into people's lives. Free shipping clearly just isn't enough for the Amazon Prime membership anymore — especially now that the price has jumped from $99 to $129. But, the digital retail giant also realizes that just because its concept isn't exciting and new anymore, it still has a large market share and the opportunity — and arguably, expectation — to be innovative.

That's why today, Prime isn't just about free shipping; it's buying into a lifestyle suite of services.

Here are just a handful of the most notable lifestyle perks consumers can leverage from a Prime membership:

- Easier Shopping with Alexa and Dash

While anyone can buy a Dot that is programmed with Alexa, Amazon's voice-activated smart-home assistant, you can only order certain Prime-approved items while using the device. A regular membership will get you access to the regular features — but for anyone who uses Amazon regularly for household items, having Alexa at your beck and call (literally) is a huge perk. You can also ask her about the day's deals, where she'll list Prime-exclusive deals.

There's also Dash, product buttons for your home that cost $4.99 a piece, but streamline household shopping for families. All you do is place one of these buttons — which can be for everything from laundry detergent to paper towels — near where the product lives in your house, and every time you need more, you press it and Prime automatically orders it for you. It's only available for certain products and brands, but it has hugely revolutionized home shopping.

- Prime Day

While the other retail giants rely on big holidays like Black Friday

That's why today, Prime isn't just about free shipping, it's buying into a lifestyle suite of services

or Cyber Monday to ramp up sales, Amazon, fittingly, decided to leverage their own base for its biggest sale of the year — Prime Day. The one-day-only global shopping event, exclusively for Prime members, is a frenzy of deals. This year, consumers purchased over 100 million products. And while Amazon won't disclose its own sales numbers, they did say that small and medium-sized businesses on the site earned over $1 billion this Prime Day.

- Prime Video

Amazon's answer to video streaming services like Netflix and Prime video allows members to stream TV shows and movies. This is technically a perk, but considering how streaming has permeated the American marketplace and psyche, it's kind of an essential for customers today. And like Netflix, Hulu, and HBO, Prime Video also produces original content — releasing popular shows like the new "Top Gear" or America's latest action-hero flick Jack Ryan. It's just another reason to buy into the Prime lifestyle.

- Whole Food Discounts

After acquiring grocery giant Whole Foods in 2017, Amazon began slashing the specialty retailer's notoriously high prices, integrating technology, and introducing its loyal customer base. Prime members could now leverage their membership to get deals on favorites throughout the store, plus an extra 10-percent off certain sale items. Before the buy-out, the organic grocer was struggling to offer competitive prices and appeal to a wider audience. The Amazon deal did just that.

- Unmatched Shopping Convenience

While the competition might be matching two-day free shipping, Amazon is slowly rolling out a suite of same-day delivery services and even 2-hour delivery for Prime members purchasing certain items. As of now, this is only available in select cities, but Seller Cloud is already set up to help qualifying clients flag their special orders and label them for priority processing and shipping. Additionally, Amazon is pushing back against the brick-and-

Amazon is pushing back against the brick and mortar competition

mortar competition that can offer 'in-store pickup' with 'Pickup Points' in certain locations as well as by opening up pop-up retail locations.

Amazon still leads the consumer experience

Today, Amazon has ingrained itself as a staple in people's lives. Consumers might have more choice than ever as the competition matches free shipping and continues to offer perks and loyalty discounts, but Amazon has the advantage of a massive consumer base and the backing of a suite of convenient lifestyle services. So while Amazon Prime might not be as lustrous as it once was, it is definitely more integrated into Prime members' lives, and it's big enough that it's not going away anytime soon.

Additionally, as Amazon continues to build out its lifestyle services, in-store pickup, and extra-fast delivery, Seller Fulfilled Prime members are only going to benefit. In creating a suite of services that make it easier than ever to shop, we see Amazon cultivating a loyal base that increasingly buys from the platform not just because it's familiar — but because it's easy. In other words, there could be a whole lot more money in your pocket.

On top of that, they'll likely roll out these services to Seller Fulfilled over time, too, making your products just as accessible on Alexa as the products in Amazon's own warehouse. SellerCloud was one of the first to integrate with the Amazon Seller Fulfilled Prime program — where products from highly-ranked sellers are shipped through the Prime program directly from the merchant's own warehouse to the customer.

At SellerCloud, we're already seeing Amazon extend its hand to successful Seller Fulfilled members with FBA Onsite. This program allows top merchants to transfer inventory to Amazon fulfillment centers where Amazon will then send them to your customers — using their Prime shipping service. Your customers are then given access to perks like 2-day and even same-day shipping.

Curious to learn how the SellerCloud platform can help you be more agile and profitable while integrated with Amazon? Get in touch to see how our tools can optimize your ecommerce business.

What Will Happen if Amazon is Forced to Change?

If you want your ecommerce business to thrive it's becoming almost mandatory that you sell on Amazon. With over 90 million Prime subscribers spending approximately $1,300 a year on the platform, business owners who are smart about leveraging Amazon's traffic have much to gain.

Amazon is the largest online retailer in the US. With same day delivery on a variety of merchandise, Amazon provides us with the convenience we crave. Where we once had to drive out to the store, find a parking space and walk through the aisles to find what we need, we can now get everything delivered to our doorstep.

Amazon's customer-centric features have revolutionized the way we shop. And the company has been rewarded for it to the tune of 800 billion dollars, making CEO Jeff Bezos the richest man in the world and arguably one of the most powerful.

But therein lies a problem. Where there is power there is often corruption. The power Amazon has over the ecommerce industry today is reminiscent of the power America's ty-coons had over the railways in the late 1800s.

Back then if you wanted to commute or transport goods you had to go through the railway system. When two very wealthy businessmen formed Northern Securities company to acquire control of all the railroad companies in the west, it caused alarm amongst the public. The United States sued the monopoly under antitrust laws and it was forced to disband.

In modern times, Amazon's policies dictate the ease (or challenge) of new third-party sellers entering the marketplace. Amazon typically releases payment to sellers every 2 weeks, but it has the liberty to withhold payment for up to 90 days. This can cause crippling cash flow problems for a small business.

Amazon might argue that unlike the railroads of yesteryear, they are not a monopoly. Traditional monopolies are known for posing a danger to the public by driving prices up. Amazon, on the other hand, drives prices down in a way that benefits consumers. Also, Amazon owns only 4% of the retail market. That's just a small sliver compared to some larger retailers.

Amazon's customer-centric features have revolutionized the way we shop

But it's a new age and monopolies don't always look the way they did in centuries before. Amazon's rising power is posing new threats that should be looked at closely.

If you want to sell goods online, more often than not you have to use Amazon's infrastructure. That's a lot of power and with power comes responsibility. Just because the behemoth seems to be wielding its power benevolently now, it may not always.

Many economists are warning that Amazon's growing power is dangerous and that the company should be split up. Regardless of whether Amazon is forced to change, it's worth exploring the impact it will have on third-party sellers.

Why Should Amazon be Split Up?

If you take a closer look, you will see that despite Amazon's relatively small share of the retail market, its power is still threatening from an antitrust perspective. Amazon owns one-third of the cloud services market with its AWS division.

Amazon has the capital and influence to do what other companies can't do in terms of research and development. And they have the size and the power to easily drive competitors out of business. Economists argue that Amazon is making it harder for new businesses to enter the marketplace and it's bad for the economy.

At the same time, Amazon has also enabled a lot of small entrepreneurs to build businesses and quickly reach captive audiences.

But it can't be denied that Amazon has potential conflicts of interest. Amazon is a private label seller on the same platform it invites third-party sellers to do business on. Amazon is often selling the same goods as third-party sellers, while at the same time collecting fees, commissions and lots of valuable data. And Amazon can charge lower prices than most third-partysellers because it doesn't have to pay its own commission fees.

Amazon also has the ability (and the incentive) to drive up the bidding prices for product ads and compete with other advertisers. When Amazon pays for ads the money just goes from its left pocket to its right pocket. Therefore, if Amazon chose to abuse its advantageous position, it would be virtually impossible for any

third-party seller to outbid them.

Another advantage Amazon has is the ability to collect data on market trends and consumer behavior. If Amazon noticed another seller's product performing well, it could conceivably manufacture a competing product and drive the third-party seller out of business.

These are the reasons why many experts argue that it's both imperative and inevitable that Amazon is broken up.

What will it mean for 3rd party sellers if Amazon is broken up?
One of the most famous antitrust cases in history was the breakup of the Bell System monopoly in 1982. At the time, AT&T was the sole provider of telephone service in the US and most of the telephone operating equipment was owned by the company's subsidiary.

When the company was ordered to divest, it was split up by geographical region into smaller companies known as the "Baby Bells."

It is possible that Amazon would be broken up in a similar fashion. Unlike eBay, which has all of its operations in a unified system, Amazon has separate systems for its US divisions and Europe divisions. For example, listing a product once on eBay makes it available anywhere in the world, whereas Amazon requires sellers

It is possible that Amazon would be broken up in a similar fashion

to register in each region and it maintains a separate database of products for each region. SellerCloud recently added support for Amazon China and Amazon Australia due to requests from its clients.

While dividing the company by geographic region is a relatively simple split, it would only slow down Amazon's dominance of international ecommerce, but it wouldn't solve the problem in the US.

But breaking up the company by service would have an even greater impact. This would mean separating Amazon the retailer from AWS, the infrastructure, and Amazon fulfillment, the shipping arm of the company. If Amazon the retailer is split off from the marketplace, its private label brands would no longer have access to the proprietary data that gives them an advantage.

This would eliminate the current conflict of interest and help create a more even playing field for third-party sellers to compete fairly.

Amazon could also employ the help of an objective third party to administer compliance. This would squash claims of conflict of interest and weaken the argument that Amazon should be broken up. Under this scenario, sellers would benefit from having a disinterested entity play referee and ensure the marketplace stays fair for the long term.

Amazon is a resilient and adaptable company. We should also consider that a split may ultimately benefit Amazon in ways that can't be foretold this early on. Regardless of how the debate ultimately plays out, there will likely be changes in Amazon's future that will affect how sellers do business.

Are you prepared to seize the opportunity?
If Amazon is affected, it's possible that there will be more space in the market for other ecommerce businesses to scale up. This could pose a tremendous earning opportunity for ecommerce retailers who are ready for it by having SellerCloud help them streamline sales across multiple sales channels. It is important to ensure that your business is as competitive as it can be now so you will be poised to take advantage once the ecommerce game changes.

Are you ready to seize this opportunity? Contact SellerCloud directly to see how our tools and expertise can help position your business to win.

There will likely be changes in Amazon's future that will affect how sellers do business

HOW THE END OF AN INTERNATIONAL SHIPPING TREATY WILL HELP U.S. SELLERS

Recently, the Trump administration announced its intention to withdraw from the Universal Postal Union (UPU). For 144 years, the multilateral treaty has been the governing force in setting international parcel shipping rates. One of the main facets of the UPU is a ranking structure that allows economically disadvantaged countries to pay discounted rates to ship packages internationally while more economically advanced countries wind up paying more. Many, including the Trump administration, claim the UPU is inherently unfair.

From the outset, the UPU's intent was to help level the playing field for developing nations by lowering the cost of doing business. Reduced shipping costs could allow developing economies to distribute their goods at a lower transactional cost and thus allow them to compete in the global economy.

Fast forward to today. Despite the fact that China is one of the world's largest economies, it is also one of the largest beneficiaries of the UPU parcel shipment discounts. According to the UPU, China is ranked as a "developing country" – a status the country uses to reap huge trade benefits.

"How is that possible?" you ask.
Simple.
The UPU's list of member countries' contribution classes (the metrics used to set international shipping rates) hasn't been updated since the 1960s – long before China's rise as a global economic superpower. While countries like the United States, Japan, and France are at the maximum contribution class rating of 50 units, China has a significantly lower rating of 25 (which is a ranking shared by smaller economies like Italy and Spain).

As a result, the combination of China's below-market international shipping costs and high volume of exports has cost the United States hundreds of millions of dollars per year. The American shipping companies (and ultimately the American taxpayers) have been left to foot the bill to make up for the difference between what China pays to export their goods and what it actually costs to deliver them stateside.

To compensate, the American retail and manufacturing sectors have spent years scrambling for ways to overcome China's growing advantages in both production and delivery. While some have succeeded, the deck is clearly stacked in China's favor.

According to the UPU, China is ranked as a "developing country"

That said, if the federal government succeeds in either renegotiating the terms of the UPU or pulling out of it altogether, the jig might finally be up. U.S. sellers may finally be in a position to outmuscle the abundance of inexpensive Chinese imports in the American marketplace.

Correcting the imbalance between domestic sales and Chinese exports

As it stands, it is cheaper to ship a small package from China to New York than it is to ship that same package across town. Combine that with the fact that many American retailers have to contend with already lower-priced, trademark-infringing Chinese products and you wind up with situations like the Mighty Mug.

This New Jersey company's self-stabilizing mug faced a direct challenge from a Chinese competitor that (dubiously) produced a cheaper version of the product and was able to deliver it to customers in the United States at a lower overall cost than the original (which was shipped from within the United States).

Pulling out of an archaic postal treaty doesn't seem like a big deal on the surface,

but it is a potential game changer for America's domestic retailers and manufacturers that have been increasingly undercut by Chinese competition – particularly in the ecommerce space. If China is forced to start paying their fair share of international shipping costs on their exports, Chinese retailers will have a harder time selling retail directly to American consumers.

For most American third-party sellers, this will be a win on multiple levels:

- In most cases, passing the increased shipping costs from China on to the American consumer will destroy their competitive price advantages over domestic goods.

- Increased shipping costs will force many Chinese retailers to choose slower shipping options that are less attractive to U.S. buyers.

- Expedited shipments from China will become prohibitively expensive for Chinese retailers already operating on paper-thin margins.

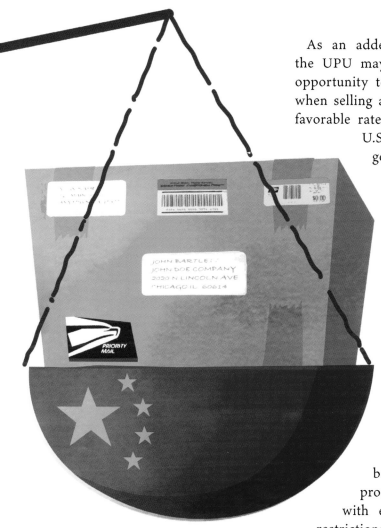

As an added bonus, withdrawal from the UPU may give American sellers the opportunity to become more competitive when selling abroad. Just as China enjoys favorable rates for shipping goods to the U.S., China can also export goods to other UPU nations like Britain and Germany at much cheaper rates than what American sellers pay. Stripping away China's competitive edge in global retail will improve the potential profitability of American exports.

How the Chinese government will respond

Gauging Chinese response has been an ongoing challenge in Trump's trade war maneuverings with China. So far, there has been a definite tit-for-tat approach employed by both sides with escalating tariffs and trade restrictions – but shipping is different.

China exports many more goods to the United States than they import. This is thanks in large part to the UPU; while it is inexpensive to ship from China to the United States, it is quite costly to ship from the United States to China. Hence, the main U.S. exports to China are high-priced luxury goods where the profit margins are large enough to offset the steep delivery costs.

Should China choose to strike back against American withdrawal from the UPU with shipping increases of their own, it probably won't matter much. Big spenders in China are unlikely to flinch at modest increases to the price of their already expensive, high-end imports. The demand will remain. As a result, existing American luxury good industries that currently rely on Chinese buyers are unlikely to see any appreciable dip in their exports.

How Chinese sellers will respond

An end to American involvement in the UPU won't mark the end of Chinese retail presence in the United States, but it will certainly alter it.

While it has become increasingly popular for Chinese retailers to sell directly to international customers through popular marketplaces like eBay or AliExpress, sell-

ers opting to remain in these channels will feel the sting of increased shipping rates and lengthy shipping times.

It is likely that Chinese retailers will increasingly opt to ship products in bulk to U.S. fulfillment centers and take advantage of services like Fulfillment by Amazon (FBA) or Shipped by Newegg. Utilizing these stateside fulfillment centers for popular items means that the goods can be delivered to customers quickly using Amazon Prime or Newegg Premier.

Some Chinese retailers are already taking advantage of this practice – especially since Chinese container shipments can take over a month to arrive in the United States by boat. Regardless of the UPU, getting inventory into the country prior to a retail sale to an American customer allows for faster turnaround time from purchase to delivery. Expect even more Chinese retailers to rely upon fulfillment center sales if shipping rates increase.

American third-party sellers that rely on Chinese imports can take advantage of this approach as well. The SellerCloud inventory management system provides users with the tools to manage these types of inbound shipments to fulfillment centers like Amazon's and Newegg's. From there, inventory is adjusted and the cost of goods sold can be efficiently tracked and analyzed.

All that said, relying on bulk exports and fulfillment centers is not without its challenges. Products sitting in warehouses are very different from those produced on demand. Fulfillment center inventory must be preconfigured and lie in wait for a potential sale. Sellers lose physical contact with their goods once they are in the hands of the fulfillment center (especially if the seller is halfway around the world). Thus, as more and more companies begin selling their inventory using fulfillment center models, the less potential there is for customization and product variety.

Amazon has taken steps to address this issue with their Seller Fulfilled Prime program. In the program's first few years, SellerCloud has already seen trends showing that many existing FBA merchants have taken advantage of Seller Fulfilled Prime as a way to add additional varieties of products to their marketplace offerings. This approach has allowed sellers to move

American third-party sellers that rely on Chinese imports can take advantage of this approach as well

beyond limitations of FBA while still taking advantage of the valuable Prime badge on their listings. What's more, since Seller Fulfilled Prime relies upon sellers' warehouses rather than Amazon's, you enjoy more control over the entire fulfillment process than overseas competitors do.

Chinese ecommerce retailers are going to have to make some significant adjustments if they wind up losing their competitive shipping advantages. Making matters worse for them, many of their remaining options for reducing shipping costs and streamlining distribution will finally be able to be matched or bested by American sellers.

Be prepared

It is important to note that withdrawal from the UPU is a yearlong process. The White House has stated that they will seek to renegotiate the terms of American involvement in the UPU during that time.

The UPU's current list of developing nations is nearly fifty years old – that predates not only China's rise as an economic juggernaut, but also modern economic cornerstones like FedEx and the internet. Regardless of whether America actually withdraws from the UPU or simply renegotiates, China's shipping rates to the United States are poised to change dramatically in the coming year.

In the meantime, there are things you can do to improve your business's competitiveness regardless of what international shipping changes may come. With the SellerCloud inventory management system, American third-party ecommerce sellers have already begun to position their businesses to compete both domestically and internationally by utilizing our tools to transition third-party ecommerce into more lucrative business models like first-party dropship sales, invoiced business-to-business sales, and private label retail.

Whatever model you choose for your company's online retail presence, SellerCloud has the tools to manage everything including inventory, invoices, shipping, and tracking every component of your cost of goods sold.

Contact us directly to learn more about how SellerCloud can help make your business stronger today and better prepared for whatever changes may come in the future.

It is important to note that withdrawal from the UPU is a yearlong process

HOW AMAZON'S NEW BRAND STRATEGY IMPACTS PRIVATE LABEL SELLERS

Resale is one of the fundamental components of retail. In nearly all cases, retail stores and online marketplaces feature branded products produced by other companies. The retailers then generate profits for themselves when those products are then sold to customers.

As an added source of revenue, most major retailers feature their own private label products, or "store brands," that compete with the market-leading, branded alternatives. These private label products are acquired directly from manufacturers and often cost less to stock than comparable big-name products.

Some popular examples include the generic over-the-counter medications offered at your local pharmacy or Walmart's Great Value, Equate, and Sam's Choice brands.

Until recently, Amazon had only tested the waters of private label retail with narrowly focused product lines. The company's AmazonBasics and Amazon Essentials lines have been promoted as high quality, value-priced options for commonplace items like batteries and charging cables.

Over the last few years however, Amazon has transitioned from dipping a toe into the private label pool to doing a full-fledged cannonball off the high dive. As of today, Amazon has increased its stable of private label brands to over 100 different offerings including products like clothing, vacuum-packed mattresses, linens, toilet paper, diapers, furniture, and a full line of office supplies.

The brand names are significantly less conspicuous than they used to be, too. Names like Presto!, Mae, Goodthreads, and Mama Bear are not easily identifiable as names of Amazon private labels (especially compared to AmazonBasics or Amazon Essentials), but that's exactly what they are.

It makes sense. On one hand, Amazon wants to promote certain products as 'good value' alternatives to pricier brand names. That's where AmazonBasics and Amazon Essentials come in.

At the same time, Amazon realizes that the name 'Amazon' doesn't do much to stir up an image of trendy fashion or chic decor. That's why Amazon opts for names like

Amazon realizes that the name 'Amazon' doesn't do much to stir up an image of trendy fashion or chic decor

Society New York and Rivet for those respective markets. They are playing to both ends of the market.

In doing so, Amazon is once again sending shockwaves through the retail world (as they so often do). Their private label sales generate higher margins and serve to leverage their sponsored listing platform by raising the bids on all competitor-sponsored product offerings. After all, Amazon doesn't just sell products, they are also using their valuable web platform's real estate to sell advertising space.

So, does Amazon's doubling-down on their private label business mean the end for other online retailers hoping to cash in on the benefits that come with selling as a private label? Not at all. Thankfully, there is still plenty of opportunity for private label sellers of all sizes.

Scaling the private label strategy

Even in the current retail market, private label sales are not the exclusive domain of the largest players like Amazon or Walmart. Selling private label products remains a lucrative way for third party ecommerce businesses to thrive in online marketplaces.

Rather than buying and reselling brand-name products from another retail company, private label sellers become the retailers themselves.

Just as is the case with the retail giants, even smaller-scale private label sellers have notable advantages over competing resellers:

- Direct relationships with product manufacturers

- Control over product packaging

- Sole responsibility for a product's marketing

- Ownership of brand trademarks and intellectual property

- Products that feature only the seller's logo

The SellerCloud inventory management system data has seen a notable increase in this trend. In most cases, the private label approach has been a boon for third party sellers of all sizes looking to make a splash in crowded ecommerce spaces.

Thankfully, there is still plenty of opportunity for private label sellers of all sizes

This shouldn't come as a surprise. As the marketplace has become saturated with more and more sellers selling the same branded popular items, it has become increasingly challenging to eke out profits. Competing for Amazon's Buy-Box clicks often times means settling for razor-thin margins which, over time, can sink your business.

It doesn't have to be that way. Selling as a private label gives sellers opportunities to increase margins by removing profit-eating markups passed on by pricey, brand-name distributor relationships.

Furthermore, control over a private label product includes control over the item as intellectual property. That means that there is also control over how the product is listed on sites like Amazon and Walmart. Your private label product gets its own listing that you can wield and market truly as your own. This means other sellers don't have the opportunity to piggyback their listings onto a private label product the same way they can with saturated, generic listings.

The advantages of selling as a private label can be quite alluring, especially as third

party sales margins continue to shrink.

What you sell as a private label matters
With Amazon's recent moves to explode onto the private seller scene, third party sellers need to be more tactical when it comes to their private label business strategies. There is still market share to grasp and money to be made, but the game has changed now that Amazon is a direct private label competitor in an increasing number of spaces.

Big consumer products players like Johnson & Johnson and Proctor & Gamble aren't worried. Consumers will continue to seek out their popular brands like Tide and Band-Aid just as they have for generations regardless of what Amazon does.

That said, your private label business probably isn't coming to the table with tens of billions of dollars in annual sales. Your approach will inevitably have to be different.

First and foremost, your private label products need to have an honest, provable added value to be able to compete. Slapping your brand on the same generic alarm clock or can opener that looks exactly the same as

Your approach will inevitably have to be different

what is sold by other retailers isn't going to cut it. There must be a level of quality and innovation that separates your private label product from the pack.

Amazon's aggressive positioning of its own private label products makes this even more important. For one thing, Amazon now features banner ads in its searches highlighting alternative products listed as "Top Rated from Our Brands." If your product can't stand up to Amazon's own options when it comes to quality and/or price, it is likely that Amazon's private label will poach the sale from yours.

Even so, just having a great product isn't enough anymore. You need the right strategies and tools to optimize your private label's profitability.

Plan ahead for the risks of selling as a private label
While there are plenty of benefits to taking the leap into private label sales, there are also a lot of risks and considerations.

For one thing, it can be easy to overlook the total cost of bringing a product to market. Private labels have to account for things like manufacturing costs as well as the marketing efforts behind both their products and brand. As an online private label seller, part of your marketing budget needs to be allocated for sponsored ads on your online marketplaces of choice. Your brand name won't matter unless sellers are exposed to it – especially early in its lifespan.

It is also helpful to market your private label products across multiple platforms. Even if Amazon is your primary sales channel, generating a presence outside of Amazon can help to legitimize your brand. SellerCloud integrates with a number of popular shopping carts like Magento and Shopify, which can simplify this process of creating your own branded website and ensure your efforts are carried out in a cost effective manner.

SellerCloud can also help merchants manage their wholesale sales of private label products. It is essential to be on a platform that will allow your brand to expand into various wholesale channels as a conventional manufacturer outside of the Amazon website. For example, you could position your private label as a dropshipping provider for Overstock or Walmart.

Even so, just having a great product isn't enough anymore

In some cases, a portion of your private label's marketing budget should be allocated to incentivizing customers to buy your product below cost. These types of sales can help raise your brand's profile and help create some traction with positive reviews. With some creativity, this can be a highly profitable move.

For example, we at SellerCloud once created a system for a client that automatically adjusted the sales price of an item based on the item's sales volume. It is important to balance between gradually building the product's sales volume while also avoiding the problem of overselling discounted inventory too quickly and missing opportunities for greater profits.

But remember, not every buying and selling experience is a positive one. Private label sellers need to account for inevitable disappointments and customer issues; this is crucial to both build and protect the brand. As such, a private label's business plan should budget for costs associated with going above and beyond for dissatisfied customers – whether it's giveaways, free returns, or other buyer-focused incentives. These promotions cost money, but they

greatly lessen the risk of a negative review and a potential hit to your future sales.

All of these factors have a direct impact on the cost of goods sold (COGS). SellerCloud tracks all of these things that factor into the COGS for accounting purposes so you can evaluate your profit per product more accurately and make strategic adjustments when needed.

Are you ready?

Amazon joining the ranks of private label retail certainly changes things for smaller competitors (let's face it, that's just about everyone at this point). However, private label selling remains a viable and profitable option for ecommerce sellers of all sizes. The key is to make sure your business decisions are both measured and assessed for maximum profitability. The SellerCloud inventory management system is the perfect companion to help your brand make a splash even in the most crowded waters.

Are you ready to start reaping the benefits of optimized private label sales? Contact SellerCloud directly to see how our tools and expertise can position your business for success.

With some creativity, this can be a highly profitable move

IS YOUR BUSINESS PREPARED FOR AMAZON'S PAY BY INVOICE SERVICE?

There are few things more frustrating than chasing down an unpaid invoice. However, invoicing remains a popular arrangement for many B2B transactions. This summer, Amazon has opened the door to a protected form of invoiced B2B selling for its millions of third party sellers.

But here's the catch: If you're selling on Amazon, you now can receive invoiced orders whether you want to or not. It doesn't matter how large or small your operation may be. It doesn't matter whether your business's cash flow can survive waiting for an invoiced payment. You're now open for invoiced sales.

Hmph. Well, can you can opt out of this new invoicing program? The answer from Amazon's Seller Central FAQ has caught many sellers off-guard: No. Amazon's mission is to offer the earth's biggest selection of products to our customers, and this includes our business customers.

To ensure a great shopping experience for Amazon Business customers, we believe that all selection should be available to them, and we believe that the services and protections we offer to sellers makes an opt-out unnecessary. This is a great opportunity for sellers and we want them to be able to participate fully.

So, Pay by Invoice is here. If you're an Amazon seller, you now accept invoiced orders from Amazon Business customers. The question is: are you prepared for what that means?

How Pay by Invoice works

Amazon's Pay by Invoice program allows qualified Amazon Business customers to choose to be invoiced for purchases rather than pay immediately at point of sale. They then have a set time period (typically net 30) to pay for their purchases in full.

What makes this program different from a typical B2B invoicing arrangement is the added peace of mind from Amazon. Sellers are guaranteed payment within 7 days past an invoice's due date, and Amazon does all the heavy lifting so a seller never has to track down a delinquent buyer. It's the least they could do since they are imposing the new invoicing policy on their entire seller base, right? For sellers who aren't thrilled about having to potentially wait 37 days to see invoice sale payments reach their accounts (or up to 59 days to receive their cash payout depending on their disbursement schedule), Amazon has a slick alternative. Sellers can choose a "Get Paid Faster" option, which will credit the

If you're an Amazon seller, you now accept invoiced orders from Amazon Business customers

balance of an invoiced and shipped order to the seller's account for a 1.5% processing fee.

What Pay by Invoice means for sellers

Many sellers seem to be responding to this new policy as an unwelcome imposition. With no way to opt out of the program entirely, sellers are left with few choices when it comes to being paid on invoiced sales. They must either wait out the invoice and settlement periods or get nickeled and dimed by Amazon to access their funds sooner.

Great. Yet another buyer-focused policy shift at the expense of third party sellers.

Not so fast.

Cash flow concerns aside, there are some truly, seller-focused benefits with this new initiative. The addition of Pay by Invoice will open up new opportunities for Amazon third party sellers. In time, this should equate to increased sales and increased profits. What's really happening here is that Amazon is expanding its Amazon Business platform by parlaying their success in the retail channel into the world of wholesale B2B.

Now, the entirety of their first and third party inventories are available to business buyers who had been previously shut out from the third party marketplace. This new direction should be a net positive for most third party sellers. Pay by Invoice and access to Amazon Business buyers represents an increase of the Amazon seller platform's overall value.

While competing ecommerce marketplaces offer sellers little more than a marketing engine to put products in front of potential buyers, Amazon is demonstrating a commitment to both expanding and simplifying the overall selling experience. Much like the value offered by Amazon's FBA services, their Pay by Invoice rollout is a feature designed to streamline the overall selling experience while also mitigating seller risk.

What's more, the SellerCloud inventory management system is already equipped to handle these new bookkeeping responsibilities and streamline the process even further. Our software reconciles the Amazon settlement report and dynamically assigns the various costs and fees (like the aforementioned "Get Paid Faster" fee) to each order and product for accurate profit and loss calculations.

For those skeptical of Amazon's dedication to handling the invoicing backend, the

This new direction should be a net positive for most third party sellers

SellerCloud inventory management system also has a transactional ledger that can track the payments to the seller's account balance by the transaction date. You can then bring that data into accounting software like QuickBooks. This way, you can make sure all of your invoice payments are accounted for, regardless of how long you have to wait to receive them. Sure, Amazon is once again changing the rules on third party sellers and introducing new fees. In exchange, they are offering business-expanding opportunities while also putting their resources behind removing some of the most annoying and potentially business-crippling barriers to entry in invoice-based B2B sales.

Time will be the ultimate judge as to the success of Pay by Invoice, but Amazon is once again taking a bold step forward in the online retail space and bringing third party sellers along for the ride (like it or not).

Contact us directly for more information on this new policy and to learn more about how the SellerCloud inventory management system is ready to support your ecommerce business through the changes. Whatever your stance on Pay by Invoice, B2B sales opportunities are here. It's time to ensure that your company is prepared to claim its piece of the market!

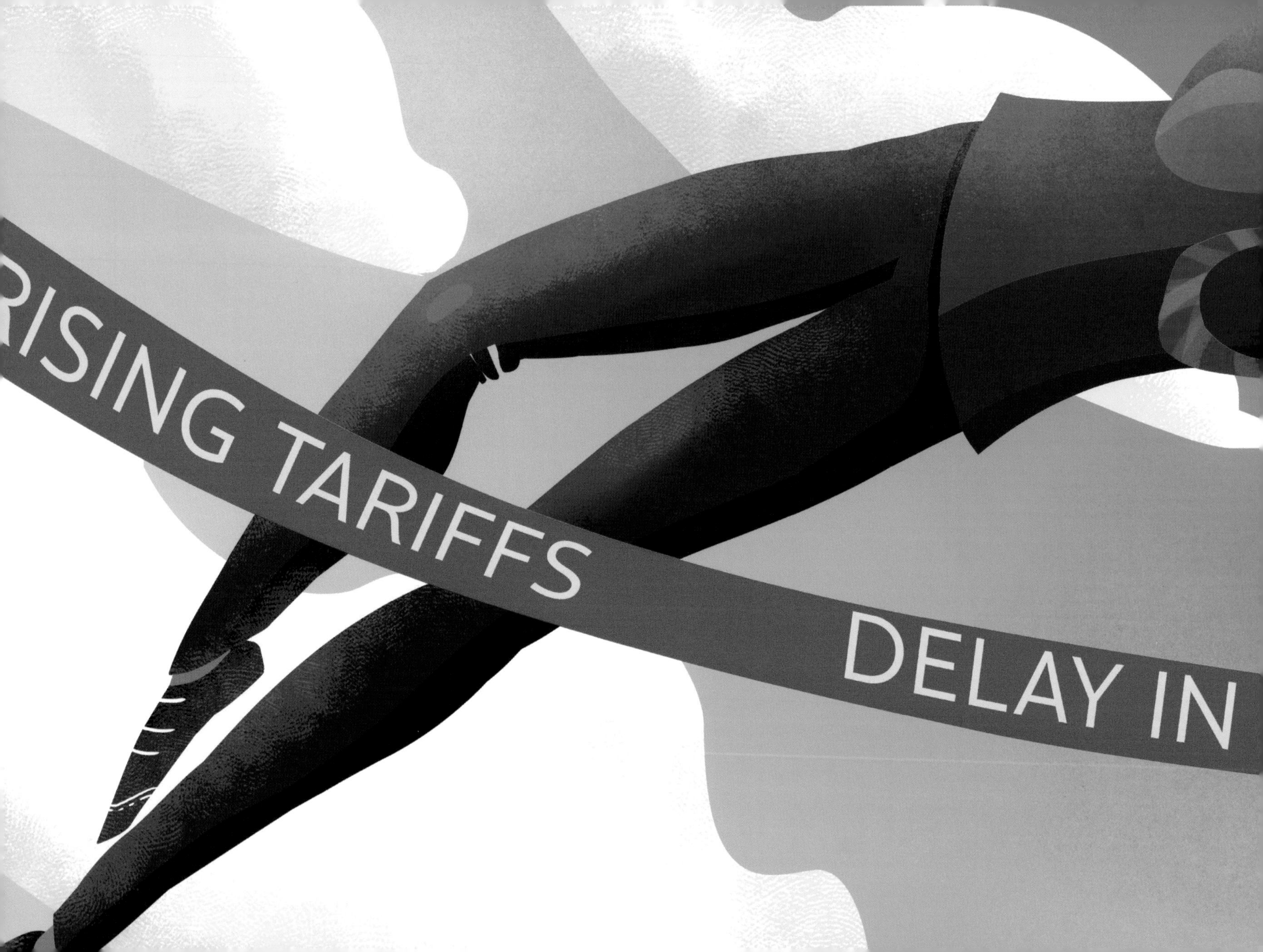
RISING TARIFFS
DELAY IN

USTOMS

WHAT DOES A US-CHINA TRADE WAR MEAN FOR YOUR ECOMMERCE BUSINESS?

This summer, America and China are continuing to ramp up a multi-billion dollar trade standoff. What started as a $34 billion opening round of tariffs between the two superpowers, quickly escalated to $200 billion. There are now even threats from President Trump that all $505 billion of Chinese imports could be hit with new tariffs.

When two of the largest economies in the planet lock horns, it's impossible for the global economy to escape the impact.

There are several ways the internet retail sector is particularly vulnerable. As this trade war plows ahead with no clear end in sight, there are a number of impacts your ecommerce business may be forced to contend with.

How will the US-China trade war affect the supply chain?

It depends. Smaller shipments sent by air from China are affected immediately. If your business relies on flying in any of the targeted Chinese goods, you are already starting to foot the bill for the new tariff costs.

Alternatively, companies that rely on high volumes of Chinese imports tend to receive goods on boats by the container-load. This means approximately 20 days of transit time to the west coast or 30 days to the east coast (plus a week or more to clear customs). It's not quick, but the process may also take longer for taxes on these types of orders to impact your bottom line – especially if you are still selling through inventory acquired prior to the new tariffs taking effect.

This is particularly relevant for many sellers. We at SellerCloud have recently seen a notable uptick in the number of customers opting for bulk, container imports rather than smaller shipments. To account for this, we have recently added container management workflow functionality to make this style of bulk import purchasing more viable and easier for sellers to deal with. Sellers can track extra third-party expenses like these tariffs (or any new ones) as a part of their cost of goods sold (COGS) calculations.

This means you can be sure that the costs are reflected correctly in the overall purchase order workflow. Sellers can easily identify the true landed cost of their inventory and calculate accurate profit figures for each product sold.

When two of the largest economies in the planet lock horns, it's impossible for the global economy to escape the impact

Will the tariffs harm your domestic sales?

The tariffs will certainly drive up the costs of imported Chinese goods and materials. Traditionally, these higher costs are passed on to customers in the form of higher prices at checkout. Conventional wisdom in sales is that higher prices are never popular with customers. When those higher prices don't come with higher profit margins, they aren't particularly popular with sellers, either.

That sounds awful, right? Not as much as you would think.

Remember, these tariffs are affecting all sellers and markets reliant upon Chinese trade, so it is probable that prices will increase across the board. Time will tell, but customers will likely continue to buy as long as the US economy remains strong. As long as you were competitive in your marketplace before the tariffs, you will likely remain so now.

What this does mean, though, is that domestic sales are likely to get a lot trickier – especially as the tariff rates continue to fluctuate. Customs is not a speedy process in the best of times. It is common for customs bills to appear well after a particular product has already been received, marketed, and sold on to a customer. This practice regularly adds a layer of ongoing flux for a purchase order's

COGS calculation. This issue will become even more volatile (and commonplace) as the ongoing tariff escalations carry on.

SellerCloud accounts for these types of changes by allowing sellers to apply the accurate COGS expenses to each transaction, even after an order has shipped – an invaluable feature in the trenches of an ongoing trade war. So now, when a whopper of a customs bill shows up after-the-fact, you can instantly apply it to the relevant purchase, recalculate the COGS, and update your profit calculations accordingly.

Will the tariffs lead to a drop in US sellers' international sales?

Given the nature of the Chinese response so far, American exports may quickly become prohibitively expensive for Chinese consumers. The tariff tit-for-tat may aim to protect domestic economies, but sellers in both America and China that rely upon sales between the two nations are going to suffer.

Increased tariffs also tend to lead to increased regulatory activity at ports of entry. This adds extra layers of red tape and processing time that will invariably lead to possible sale-killing delays. Expect to hear about many more packages being held up in customs for inspections and/or the assessment of additional fees. Over time, international customers who need or want their purchases in a timely fashion will likely start to consider other options for the extra degree of certainty – even if that means extra cost.

Broadening the scope beyond China, rising international anti-American sentiment and consumer-level actions like boycotts of American goods could also slow exports for American retailers. Furthermore, China is just one of the many nations facing new American tariff provocations. Canada, Mexico, and many European nations are also in the crosshairs.

All told, exporters are in for a rough ride as long as these types of trade wars continue to escalate and the current trend of American economic protectionism remains. Sellers that prioritize international sales will need to pay close attention to these developments in the coming weeks and months and adjust accordingly.

That said, it is worth noting that SellerCloud data shows that international sales do not make up an especially large

Sellers that prioritize international sales will need to pay close attention to these developments

percentage of the sales conducted by most American ecommerce retailers. For most online sellers, international orders may slow, but the impact shouldn't be insurmountable as long as domestic sales remain strong.

How will the tariffs affect goods sold directly from Chinese sellers to US consumers?

A growing number of the top sellers in Americans' favorite ecommerce marketplaces are originating from Chinese-based operations. These Chinese sellers have been able to offer large volumes of low-priced products at paper-thin margins on some of the leading internet retail sites like Amazon, eBay, and Ali Express. For US customers willing to endure longer shipping times, the savings compared to domestic alternatives can be dramatic. At least these tariffs will change all that and help out the average American seller, right?

Unfortunately, not yet.

Normally, packages priced lower than $800 are exempt from duty, so they would be unaffected by the current tariffs. The majority of the Chinese products sold to US consumers fall well below that threshold. If the US government is serious about leveling the playing field for domestic businesses and protecting the US marketplace from cheap knockoffs of American intellectual property (as has been the oft-stated intent), this may change.

The reality is, even with these new tariffs, the playing field still isn't level. A Chinese seller can typically sell a product directly from a local Chinese manufacturer to an American consumer at a lower cost than an American seller can domestically. Add to that, the cost of an ePacket shipment from China to a US residential customer is dramatically cheaper than if a US seller used US shipping options to send the same package to a customer down the street. It may not seem like it's getting any easier to be an online retailer these days. Between trade wars, revised internet sales tax rules, and even online marketplace policy shifts, the winds of change are blowing.

Don't fret. Online retail will remain a profitable avenue for the foreseeable future. You just need the right partner to maximize your selling potential. SellerCloud has you covered. Contact us directly to see how our platform can optimize your ecommerce business and ensure that you are always prepared for changes like these as well as any other shifts in the online retail landscape.

> The reality is, even with these new tariffs, the playing field still isn't level

HOW THE SUPREME COURT'S SALES TAX DECISION WILL IMPACT YOUR ECOMMERCE BUSINESS

The recent Supreme Court ruling in South Dakota v. Wayfair Inc. is poised to complicate the way online retailers, big and small, do business. How will your business respond?

Until now, the law of the land has been that online retailers could avoid charging sales tax to customers in states where the seller did not have a physical presence, or nexus. For instance, if your business is located in New York and you were selling a product to a customer in Marietta, Oklahoma, you could forgo adding the combined 10% state and local sales taxes to the purchase price.

Unsurprisingly, customers in high-tax states have shown increased motivation to order from third-party marketplaces to avoid paying the additional sales taxes on their purchases (despite oft-ignored state laws that require customers to report and pay use taxes after the fact).

In the case of Amazon, over 50% of all sales are from third-party sellers. These sellers have been able to take advantage of the "physical presence" loophole as a way to undercut the local brick and mortar retailers in the states that collect sales taxes.

That loophole is now closed.
South Dakota v. Wayfair overturns the physical presence precedent (set by 1992's Quill Corp v. North Dakota) and strips away these online interstate sales tax benefits enjoyed by both sellers and buyers. All online sellers are now expected to collect the appropriate sales tax on every transaction.

This raises some important questions and logistical hurdles that all ecommerce businesses need to be concerned with.

How are the states going to respond?
Supreme Court rulings are not like legislative actions that can take months or even years to roll out. When the court reaches a decision, it's binding federal law.

This is a special case where the online sales tax issue has now been tossed into the hands of the individual states. It is up to them to enforce the court's ruling and begin collecting on this new avenue for sales tax revenue if and how they choose to do so. In most cases, this will mean drafting and passing legislation to adjust state tax codes. The decision is technically federal law now, but it may take some time for states to put it into action.

South Dakota v. Wayfair overturns the physical presence precedent

Some states will fast track this process by borrowing the framework of the existing South Dakota law (which is complicated by sales volume and transaction value thresholds), while other states may take their own approaches.

Ultimately, it is likely many states will take a cue from states like Pennsylvania and Washington that already have laws on the books holding the marketplaces (like Amazon and Walmart) accountable for the sales tax collection on their platforms instead of chasing after the individual third-party sellers. After all, there's more to be gained by regulating the whole pond rather than trying to wrangle each of the individual fish swimming in it – especially when those fish account for over half of all ecommerce sales.

One thing is for sure: states will certainly be weighing how much they want to poke the bear that is interstate commerce law. This will not be the last time the sales tax issue has its day in court.

Regardless, online sellers will need to stay abreast of these developments in every state they ship to.

What does South Dakota v. Wayfair mean for individual sellers?
Headaches.
The South Dakota v. Wayfair decision means that sellers must charge, collect, and document the proper amount of sales tax for each state and jurisdiction where they sell to. What's more, sellers will need to file sales tax returns with each state that they do business with each year.

There is hope that states will take steps to simplify the process as Pennsylvania and Washington already have, but there will certainly be states that do not.

Many states already have complicated sales tax structures that differentiate between types of products, where the sale originates, and even what specific county or city the customer lives in. This isn't just a case of sellers having to become familiar with a few dozen state sales tax rates, there are literally thousands of possible combinations of state and local sales tax considerations to account for.

I won't sugar-coat it – interstate sales are going to be more complicated than ever before.

This will not be the last time the sales tax issue has its day in court

What impact will South Dakota v. Wayfair have on online sales?

For customers whose primary reason for shopping online is dodging sales tax, the South Dakota v. Wayfair ruling all but eliminates their motivation for clicking the 'Check Out' button. Third-party sellers will certainly feel the impact on their bottom lines.

That said, one of the major selling points of online retail still remains untouched – convenience. If your ecommerce operation offers a reliable and streamlined purchasing experience for customers, this is a storm you will be able to weather. Just make sure that you have your bookkeeping in order!

Are there any tools or solutions that help sellers deal with this issue?
Yes!
The SellerCloud platform has built-in integration with TaxJar to help with this very type of issue. The TaxJar service has its own direct integration features with some of the most widely used online marketplaces (Amazon, eBay, Walmart). However, when combined with the SellerCloud platform and its wide range of seller channel integrations, TaxJar's value increases exponentially.

With a linked TaxJar account, SellerCloud ensures that each of your orders includes the exact, up-to-date sales tax amounts for each state and domestic locale you ship to. Come tax time, you can even file your sales tax returns automatically in most states.

This means that while new sales tax rules will certainly affect your online business, they don't have to place undue burdens on your time or sanity.

Want to know more about how SellerCloud can help navigate your business through these changes (and whatever other policy changes may come down the pike)? Request a live demo to see how our software can streamline your online sales and ensure you are always optimizing both your profits and compliance.

How are sellers reacting now?
This may be the most interesting and important trend to watch.
So far, most sellers are doing...well... nothing.
In the short term, this makes sense. Being one of the first ecommerce businesses in your marketplace to comply with the new sales tax rules (most of which aren't even

One of the major selling points of online retail still remains untouched

formalized yet), puts you at a competitive disadvantage.

When customers are given a choice of two comparable products, price is often the determining factor. Your timely addition of a sales tax charge won't do you any favors. Let's face it; customers aren't lining up to reward your sense of civic duty. Plain and simple, being one of the first sellers in your market to tack on additional sales tax means you'll probably lose sales.

Conversely, playing 'wait and see' as the states shake out their responses to South Dakota v. Wayfair is a more measured and practical approach. While there is certainly a risk of a state audit exposing your failure to collect the appropriate sales taxes, the potential hit to your sales is far riskier at this stage in the game.

If past practice is any indication, online sales tax enforcement has traditionally been quite lax. For example, even before this most recent ruling, sellers who participated in the Fulfillment by Amazon (FBA) service technically had a physical presence in every state with an Amazon warehouse. That means they were obligated to collect sales tax on all qualifying transactions involving customers in those states.

The reality is that hardly any FBA customers took this compliance very seriously or received any punitive action for their neglect.

That's not to say the states have sat idly by. In 2017, several states came together to offer an FBA tax amnesty program to try and raise both awareness and their owed taxes. Some states, like Massachusetts and California, have stepped up enforcement and collection efforts targeting individual online marketplace sellers (as opposed to states like South Carolina that are focusing more on the marketplaces themselves).

In the end, states continue to vary in both their willingness and resources to enforce online retail sales taxes. Especially in the case of smaller sellers, the cost to pursue back taxes often outweighs the funds being sought.

In the face of the South Dakota v. Wayfair ruling, sellers need to weigh the costs versus the risks of compliance. At this stage, the cost of becoming compliant could mean filing dozens if not hundreds of additional tax

States continue to vary in both their willingness and resources to enforce online retail sales taxes

documents each year as well as losing out to noncompliant sellers on countless sales opportunities. For many third-party sellers (especially those who conduct the majority of their online sales away from large, targeted, third-party marketplace platforms like Amazon) this cost very well may outweigh the price of having to possibly pay missed sales taxes and fines down the line.

Whatever path forward you choose, the lesson here is clear: the third-party online retail space is ever evolving. Are your online sales both prepared for and protected against these types of political and economic changes? Contact us at SellerCloud directly to learn about how our platform is the ideal way to ensure your ecommerce business makes the right decisions when it comes to being agile, profitable, and compliant.

PROPOSITION 65 AND HOW TO PROTECT YOUR BUSINESS FROM COMPLIANCE VIOLATIONS

From the outside looking in, some people might think that once ecommerce skills and processes are mastered, then they will attain success. But if you've been in business for any length of time, you've likely realized there is more to being a successful seller than meets the eye.

Ecommerce is governed by a number of rigorous regulations, such as Proposition 65, so in addition to sales, marketing, and inventory, compliance is just as important. With regulations constantly being amended and new regulations regularly being added to the books, staying informed and keeping your company compliant can be a challenge. Although it can sometimes feel daunting, mastering compliance is imperative to maintaining the health and longevity of your business which, especially as it grows, it's more likely to become a target.

In this article, we'll discuss a compliance issue that may force you to change how you do business. Read on to find out what the latest amendments to Proposition 65 may mean for your company.

What is Proposition 65?
Proposition 65 is an initiative that was voted into law in California in 1986. Formally known as Safe Drinking Water and Toxic Enforcement Act of 1986, it was put into place to help California consumers make more informed purchases in the wake of growing concerns about exposure to toxic chemicals.

Effective in 1988, the law requires California to publish a list of chemicals known to cause cancer or reproductive toxicity.

There are over 900 chemicals on the list with more being added all the time. Under the law, businesses with more than 10 employees are required to warn consumers of the presence of hazardous chemicals in their products. And it's important to be aware that the nature of the consumer warnings is ever-evolving.

Prior to the recent amendments, most companies stayed in compliance by providing a broad warning on their products, stating something along the lines of "This product may contain a hazardous chemical that may cause health risks." Many companies took a cautious approach and applied a broad and general warning label to almost everything just to be safe. But if everything has a warning it becomes meaningless.

In 2016, the law was reformed with the in-

There is more to being a successful seller than meets the eye

tent to make Proposition 65 warnings more useful to the public and to provide guidance to business as to how and where to provide warnings. The new amendments regarding warning labels are effective as of August 30, 2018. The new regulations apply to any products manufactured after this date that are sold in California.

The amendments make Proposition 65 far more enforceable. Under the new warning regulations, to be protected under safe harbor a business must place specific warnings on product labels and on websites including the name of the hazardous chemical and the health risk it presents.

For example, "This product can expose you to hazardous chemicals including, [insert name of chemical], which is known by the state of California to cause [insert health risk]".

The new law not only requires that warnings be more specific, but also that they be provided in other languages under certain circumstances. If your company provides any marketing communications or assembly instructions in foreign languages, then you must provide warnings in those languages as well. SellerCloud has a feature to attach an instruc-

tions file to a product. Emails can then be sent to the customer with a link to the instructions, immediately upon purchase, so that they are aware of all of the warnings.

In short, not only do the new amendments make Proposition 65 more enforceable but also more cumbersome from a business owner's perspective.

What do the changes to Proposition 65 mean for sellers?

In general, larger businesses are at greater risk when it comes to compliance enforcement. For example, sales tax is only enforced on businesses doing over $100,000 in New Jersey. Similarly, Proposition 65 only applies to businesses with over 10 employees. So, if you are a large enterprise it might be in your best interest to be extra-thorough in your compliance efforts.

If your business is found to be in violation of Proposition 65, the ramifications can be costly. A court may order your business to stop committing the violation. For some businesses, this might mean closing your listings on Amazon and taking a significant cut in revenue.

Even more threatening, a business found in

Larger businesses are at greater risk when it comes to compliance enforcement in general

violation of Proposition 65 may also be subject to civil penalties of up to $2,500 per day for each violation. For some businesses a Proposition 65 violation could mean financial ruin.

If you are cautious and apply the new warnings to ensure you are in compliance, you risk scaring customers away from your products. It is already a challenge to get customers to part with their hard-earned money in exchange for your product. You probably already have a long list of objections to overcome to make the sale and this could make it that much harder.

The new warnings may raise objections that are harder to overcome than any other. Unless you're selling tobacco, customers usually aren't eager to purchase products that cause cancer or put their expectant offspring at risk. So, it's possible that applying the warning labels may cause sales to plummet.

The good news is that right now the regulations only apply to companies that do business in California, but to be clear, your business doesn't have to be located in California for the law to affect you. Regardless of where you're located, if you sell products in California, Proposition 65 applies to your business.

Moreover, Proposition 65 only applies to goods sold in California, it's important to stay adaptable. California is known for leading the nation when it comes to legislation. For example, several states have adopted California's strict vehicle emission standards. Based on the recent history of how legislation has developed in the US, it is likely that other states will start imposing regulations similar to Proposition 65. This means that this challenge isn't going away anytime soon. And in fact, it may grow in scope. Therefore, it's important to stay informed and prepared in order to protect your business.

How Can Sellers Protect Their Business?
It's important that you are working with suppliers that you trust to inform you of the presence of any hazardous materials. If you are manufacturing your own private label products, you may want to order laboratory tests for your products so you know exactly what you're selling and what you need to do to comply.

If you're currently selling a product with hazardous chemicals, you may want to consider finding alternative ways to manufacture the product without the harmful chemicals. This strategy would allow you to list and ship the product without the dire warning labels so you

wouldn't have to worry about losing sales.

And even better, if your business is one of the first to the market to provide a cleaner, more health-conscious solution to an existing problem for your customer base, this feature could give you a huge competitive advantage.

Although the Prop 65 amendments are creating challenges in the short term, the changes you make to adapt may result in long term gains.

It is worth noting that switching suppliers or finding new ways to manufacture your product may prove costly on the front end. However, it may save you money and hassles in the future. If other states adopt similar regulations to Proposition 65, adjusting now will save you from struggling with compliance challenges when other states follow California's lead.

But what if manufacturing your product without hazardous materials is impossible or switching suppliers is truly cost prohibitive? What can you do to protect the success of your business?

If you are in a situation where you need to provide warning labels, catalog software can help. With SellerCloud, you can mark the information once on a product and send the information to many different channels. All of the major marketplaces from Amazon, eBay, Walmart and Jet, to Houzz and Overstock, have attributes in their catalog to flag items as subject to Proposition 65 and also to include the warning message. Leveraging our software will help you to stay in compliance without slowing down operations.

Another avenue that's worth considering in light of the new warning laws is to cease doing business in California. Ever since the new Proposition 65 amendments started in August 2018, some sellers have cancelled all orders shipping to California.

Unfortunately, this is only a short-term fix. Cancelling too many orders will negatively affect your seller metrics and Amazon will likely penalize your business. SellerCloud has another option: to flag the product with a warning so that the warehouse won't ship it out without acknowledging the warning. That gives the warehouse a chance to ensure that all products have the appropriate labels on them before they leave the warehouse. You can also go a step further with an 'after order plugin' whereby you can set business rules to determine when to add the warnings, taking into

account other factors as well.

And there is still hope. Amazon has added regional shipping templates that take a customer's location into account before shipping. Moreover, they have been testing the capability to restrict sales of products to certain states. It is possible that in the future this may provide a good solution for sellers. If your business doesn't sell in California, then you can avoid applying the new warning labels and still stay in compliance.

Until it is possible to restrict your products from being sold in California, Proposition 65 will likely change how you do business. But now that you're informed, your business has a better chance of navigating through these changes successfully. Compliance is an ever-present challenge for ecommerce sellers that is constantly evolving. It's easy to fall behind. In addition to Proposition 65 regulations, there are MAP Price requirements and channel restrictions to manage.

Don't leave your business at risk for compliance violations. Contact SellerCloud and find out how you can leverage our software to automate some of your compliance processes so you can focus on growing your business.

Ever since the new Proposition 65 amendments started in August, some sellers are cancelling all orders shipping to California

WHAT AMAZON'S "AUTO-AUTHORIZED RETURNS" POLICY MEANS FOR YOUR BUSINESS

Selling on Amazon can be a boon for your ecommerce business. However, it's easy to get caught by surprise if you're not paying close attention to the company's ever-evolving policies.

One of the most severe changes in recent memory is Amazon's move toward auto-authorized, pre-paid returns. For unprepared sellers, failure to address this particular set of procedures will inevitably become a costly mistake.

Amazon's official policy lays out this new returns process:

- The seller is notified that a return has been initiated and a return shipping label has been automatically created.

- The seller is charged for the shipping costs once the label is accepted by the carrier (in theory – more on this later).

- Once the returned package arrives, the seller has two business days to process the refund manually, otherwise, Amazon automatically issues the customer a refund.

Prior to this change, if an Amazon customer sought to return a purchase from a third party seller, the seller had the ability to authorize the return request. As a seller, this opened a dialogue and gave you an opportunity to come to a satisfactory resolution with a dissatisfied buyer before a return and refund process was carried out.

Those days are over. With auto-authorized returns, buyers now have the ability to initiate returns and generate return shipping labels without interacting with the seller at all.

Presently, should a seller have an issue with one of these auto-authorized returns, the only real recourse is a SAFE-T claim that may or (more likely) may not result in a favourable seller outcome. While waiting for the outcome of such an appeal, the seller could be out both their unreturned product and the money from the sale.

On Amazon's "Appeal a return" page, it doesn't take much reading between the lines to realize where the company's allegiances lie in these instances:

"To maintain customer trust, consider refunding the undisputed amount of a return

It's easy to get caught by surprise if you're not paying close attention to the company's ever-evolving policies

request to the buyer before filing an appeal. Waiting to refund the customer until an outcome of the appeal has been granted increases the wait time for the buyer to receive their refund."

Now more than ever Amazon is clearly leaning into the belief that "the customer is always right."

Ideally, this buyer-focused returns policy should lead to increased customer confidence in third parties. Amazon users can now purchase from the site's independent sellers with the same perceived level of service and security as they experience from buying directly from Amazon. If a sale or product doesn't live up to expectations (for virtually any reason), the return process is executed quickly and refunds are issued in a timely manner. It's not as fast as bringing a return to the customer service desk at a retailer like Walmart, but it's close and arguably more convenient.

The data would suggest that customers agree. My company, SellerCloud, which represents 3% of the third-party sellers on Amazon, has seen a notable uptick in returns since this new policy was instituted. From our records, customers are clearly taking advantage of the new, simpler auto-authorized return system.

What auto-authorized returns mean for sellers

As with many of Amazon's seller policy changes, this shift seems to produce an increasingly positive buyer experience while creating a more burdensome and generally negative seller experience.

Nevertheless, Amazon remains a buyer-focused company with an enormous user base. If sellers want access to Amazon's customers, they must jump through the hoops to create a customer experience that complies with Amazon's policies. Full stop.

In the case of auto-authorized returns, that means additional responsibilities and burdens that can create havoc for your ecommerce workflow. Some of the potential issues include:

- Missing the 48-hour return deadline

  Amazon has created a very narrow window for sellers to process returns. If sellers want to protect themselves against incorrect or fraudulent returns,

Ideally, this buyer-focused returns policy should lead to increased customer confidence in third parties

they must be equipped to handle this lightning-quick turnaround time.

What's more, there is no telling when an automatically authorized return is actually going to be shipped back by a customer. Sure, Amazon sends an email to notify sellers of initiated returns, but from there, the waiting game begins. This means return packages could simply start appearing at your doorstep weeks after the initial RMA email from Amazon. Regardless of this delay, you must be ready to process the returns whenever they show up on the doorstep.

While we can't change the policy, SellerCloud has features that ensure sellers are best equipped to handle an automatically-approved return. Among these are the ability to import and track customer-created RMAs from Amazon. This way, when a return package arrives, you can simply scan the shipping label's tracking number and instantly access the RMA record. From there, just verify the items and process the refund. The whole return can be handled quickly with the fewest number of steps and with the least number of potential issues as possible. No more auto-authorized returns slipping through the cracks!

- Returns lost in transit

If a return is lost during the return shipping process, a refund still automatically goes through to the customer. From there, it is entirely up to you the seller to file a claim with the carrier to recoup the loss.

This means that the seller has lost the product, the money from the original sale, and now the time involved in pursuing a lost package claim. Buyers win. Sellers lose.

- Buyers that game the return shipping process

Technically, when customers return items for reasons other than defects or seller error, they are responsible for return shipping costs. However, rather than selecting one of these options during a return (i.e. no-longer-wanted, changed mind, accidental order, or found a better price), customers learn

This means return packages could simply start appearing at your doorstep

to opt for other options that put the shipping cost burden back on the seller.

Sellers can appeal wrongful shipping charges with a SAFE-T claim, but all it takes is a mysterious ding or scratch for a customer to claim receipt of a damaged item and win an appeal.

- Buyers return the wrong item

Amazon's seller forums are filled with accounts of sellers receiving returned items that are nowhere near what they shipped to their customers. With auto-authorized returns, this type of dishonest buyer behaviour is that much easier to get away with.

Sellers used to have more discretion in the acceptance of returns and could more easily hold a refund in these cases. If a seller returned a knock-off instead of an original or a damaged item instead of a new one, the seller had the time to comfortably make a case before any money changed hands.

Not anymore. Amazon wants sellers to get refunds back to dissatisfied custom-ers as quickly as possible. Sellers are left holding the bag with only a narrow 48-hour window to verify and prove customer errors or dishonesty before the refund is remitted automatically.

In most of these situations, the buyer winds up with both the unreturned item and a refund. From there, the only option left for you the seller is to file an appeal with Amazon and hope for the best. That said, don't get your hopes up. After all, it's always easier to hold a refund than get one back that has already been paid.

- Incorrect shipping weight

Sellers must ensure their packages and products are properly weighed. Amazon uses the weight on the Product Detail page to determine the cost of pre-paid return shipping. If the weight of the product you shipped to a customer is higher, expect an extra shipping charge to cover the difference. If there is no shipping weight provided, Amazon goes with a default weight of 4.9 lb.

Left unchecked, these types of miscal-

In most of these situations, the buyer winds up with both the unreturned item and a refund

culations can lead to returns that further hurt your bottom line.

- Paying for unused shipping labels but not receiving returned items

According to Amazon, "Your account will be charged for the return label cost only when the buyer returns the package to the carrier." However, this is proving to not always be the case. Sellers have been reporting instances where they were charged for pre-paid shipping labels, but following up with the tracking numbers returns the status "Label Created, not yet in system" – the packages were never actually shipped but the seller was still charged.

If you are not monitoring Amazon's auto-created, pre-paid return shipping labels closely, you may wind up paying for shipping services that were never actually used by the buyer. Sellers must pay extra close attention to the shipping expenses in their settlement reports to avoid unnecessary losses.

As a way to simplify things, SellerCloud automatically tracks these shipping expenses as part of a seller's profit and loss reporting. This makes it less likely that unused return labels will go unnoticed and wind up costing you.

Easing the burden of these new seller responsibilities

What these scenarios boil down to is that, when it comes to returns, time is of the essence. Sellers need to stay on top of these automatically authorized returns and the resulting shipping labels to avoid suffering frustrations, losses, and potentially business-damaging consequences.

For the foreseeable future, these are Amazon's rules of the road. If you want to sell on Amazon, be prepared to comply or else.

The best sellers do so by putting systems in place with reliable tools, convenient tracking, and efficient workflows so that both Amazon's policies and their business's interests can be met.

If your business needs help to keep up with Amazon returns or you just don't know where to start, please contact SellerCloud directly to learn more about how we can save you time and help protect against unnecessary losses.

If you want to sell on Amazon, be prepared to comply or else

In the not too distant past, online daily deal sites were all the rage. Bargain-hunting customers would habitually scour their inboxes and hammer the refresh button of their favorite sites to score what they hoped would be once-in-a-lifetime discounts.

The experience was equal parts QVC and Cyber-Monday for both the loyal and casual deal site shoppers alike. Every day, a very select collection of merchandise was marked down by such a substantial degree that quantities and time had to be limited. It was "Act now!" impulse buying at its finest. Word got out about these sites and their popularity grew.

As much as customers loved these sites, ecommerce sellers loved these sites even more. To be featured on a daily deal site was a marketing boon that could potentially grow a customer base, brand awareness and allow sellers to unload large quantities of inventory (especially perishable, refurbished, or outdated merchandise that was otherwise difficult to move) at the same time.

Then came Groupon. Once hailed by Forbes and CNBC as one of (if not the) fastest growing companies ever, the group coupon site created an entirely new way to link local businesses to local consumers through the combination of networking and scale. Each day a new service or piece of merchandise would appear on the site at a noteworthy discount. If a certain number of customers purchased the deal within the allotted 24 hours, the promotion would be valid. If too few customers bought in, the deal vanished into thin air.

The Groupon business model was simple: Companies were enticed to offer steep discounts and great deals based on the promise of group purchasing. Higher sales volumes and the prospect of repeat, full-price business would (theoretically) offset smaller margins.

Faith was so strong in the Groupon social commerce model that the company earned a staggering $6 billion buyout valuation from Google (an offer Groupon turned down).

It didn't last. Groupon and the larger daily deal craze have struggled to endure as both businesses and customers have increasingly lost their enthusiasm for the dedicated deal-of-the-day site.

This phenomenon has led to a massive drop-off in both sales and the number of these sites still active today. Most have either had to

In the not too distant past, online daily deal sites were all the rage

sell out to larger marketplaces (like woot! did in 2010) or close up shop completely.

These transitions haven't always been smooth, either. In 2016, New York-based deal site Choxi mysteriously shut down leaving buyers and sellers alike in the dark about the statuses of their orders and payments. The company filed for bankruptcy in January of 2017 and many shoppers and merchants were left empty-handed. Incidents like this one and this summer's Chapter 11 bankruptcy filing by Tanga have helped to fuel a growing seller exodus from the daily deal marketplaces.

It hasn't been all bad. Several of the most influential players in the daily deal space, like Groupon, have been able to cling to life by drastically altering their business models to better mirror current consumer trends.

Taking the pulse of daily deal sites today
Today's online retail customer expects variety and on-site comparison-shopping – two elements conspicuously absent from the daily deal site model.

Instead, customers are flocking to large retail websites where choice and price options abound. To make matters worse for the daily deal sites, these large online retailers have adopted many of the best parts of the daily deal model and integrated them into their home pages. For instance, Amazon features both daily and lightning deals that entice customers with large discounts, limited quantities, and time-sensitive availability. Along those same lines, eBay's Deals page highlights a series of the site's best time and quantity sensitive bargains each day.

What buyers don't see is the way some of these sites use a subsidy model to help drive down consumer costs while protecting sellers' margins. For example, both eBay and NewEgg have deal programs that offer customers discounted prices, but when an item sells, the sellers are credited back the some or all of the discounted amount. To make life easier, SellerCloud is equipped to handle these transactions and to ensure that the profit and loss calculations can be imported seamlessly into Quickbooks.

The concept of a dedicated daily deal site has been rendered all but obsolete thanks in large part to the implementation of these daily deal variations onto the front pages of established ecommerce marketplaces. For most sellers, participating in deal promotions on

These transitions haven't always been smooth, either

marketplaces that they already use and trust is preferable to competing for space on ones they don't – especially if the deal discounts are subsidized.

For customers, the take-it-or-leave-it presentation of a daily deal site's limited inventory just doesn't have the same excitement or appeal it once did. Daily deal sites involve extra clicks and hoops to jump through for users that already have established online retail routines. The largest ecommerce retailers know this and continue to press their advantage.

Despite all this, dedicated daily deal sites do still exist. SellerCloud continues to offer plugins for and integrations with some of the most popular deal sites. What's more, SellerCloud has created a versatile set of mapping tools that allow users to easily integrate with other retail sites (whether they are of the daily deal variety or otherwise). Users can import an order file from any site and integrate it into their existing order and tracking workflows. These orders can even be exported into a wide variety of popular formats.

Interest may be waning, but there is still money to be made on daily deal sites if they are part of a larger, marketplace diversification plan – a process the SellerCloud inventory management system aims to make as easy and painless as possible.

That said, these sites are clearly not ideal places to sell exclusively. Major problems persist for the remaining daily deal site holdouts. The same factors that led to massive drop-offs in consumer interest nearly a decade ago are still lingering today:

- Deals increasingly feature older, outdated products – often one or more model years behind current offerings.

- Deals have become even less impressive as online retail prices have fallen and selection has grown on the most popular online marketplaces like Amazon and Walmart.

- Many deal sites have an over-reliance on refurbished merchandise.

- Unfamiliar shopping cart and purchasing experiences are a turn-off for the average online shopper.

- Purchasing discounted services results in substandard service or challenges in

There is still money to be made on daily deal sites

having deals honored.

- Sites feature frustrating terms of service.

- Sites impose restrictive limits on returns.

Considering these factors, it should be no surprise that many deal-of-the-day sites have either lost their luster or gone out of business completely.

Groupon survives
Groupon, since turning down Google's $6 billion in 2012, has changed course and become a full-fledged ecommerce marketplace. The evolution hasn't been the easiest. According to reports this July, the former daily deal giant was valued at under $2.5 billion and looking for a buyer.

Sellers are also feeling Groupon's pain. SellerCloud data shows that sellers are experiencing declining sales numbers since the summer. Alexa traffic ranks took a notable dip as well.

These days Groupon is very much a company in transition; but that doesn't change the fact that there is still money to be made as a seller on the platform.

In fact, Groupon's ability to pivot is the very thing that has likely prevented its demise even while many competing daily deal sites are gasping for air. As such, Groupon is continuing to press ahead with a new vision that has strong implications for online sellers.

So when Groupon founder and former CEO Andrew Mason flippantly refers to the site's current iteration as "a marketplace of coupons," that's not necessarily a bad thing for ecommerce businesses. Groupon is continuing to try to find ways to remain relevant and fresh in the eyes of consumers. Most recently, the company has announced a new partnership with movie theater giant AMC as well as other deliberate shifts further away from their daily deal roots.

One of the foundations for these most recent moves was the 2015 addition of Groupon Stores. In its initial form, Groupon used to physically acquire the inventory it sold and then ship orders out to buyers directly. Conversely, Groupon Stores works more like more a traditional third-party ecommerce arrangement. Sellers post their inventory to the marketplace, process and ship merchandise

These days Groupon is very much a company in transition

themselves, and pay a percentage of each sale back to Groupon.

Is it the biggest and best marketplace out there right now? No, but Groupon is very much a viable option for third-party sellers looking to diversify their web presence beyond the larger sites like Amazon and eBay.

The SellerCloud inventory management system makes working with Groupon's marketplace more convenient. To start with, SellerCloud's integration with Groupon includes several key features to ensure everyone – from sellers to buyers – has a smooth purchasing experience including:

- Channel invoicing to reconcile payments both from customers and to Groupon

- The ability to import Groupon chargebacks and update orders accordingly

- Embedded protocols to ensure packages are shipped in accordance with Groupon and customer specifications

- Support for Groupon Canada

- Delivery status tracking to assist with service level agreement (SLA) compliance

- Inventory management safeguards like the ability to create manual reserves and set up triggered releases

Daily deal sites:
a diagnosis, not a postmortem
So to answer the question: No, daily deal sites are not dead. While many are struggling, sites like Groupon that are willing to adapt and be reborn in line with current market trends should be a hopeful sign that there is still potential left in the core model.

As an ecommerce seller, establishing positive relationships with daily deal sites and their customers remains a worthwhile strategy as long as your expectations are realistic. The boom of 2010 is long gone, but you can still position your company as a profitable player in the space – especially if you focus on the strongest, most reliable options like Groupon.

Contact us directly to explore ways you can incorporate daily deal marketplaces into your current ecommerce workflow smoothly and with minimal risk.

Sites like Groupon are willing to adapt and be reborn in line with current market trends

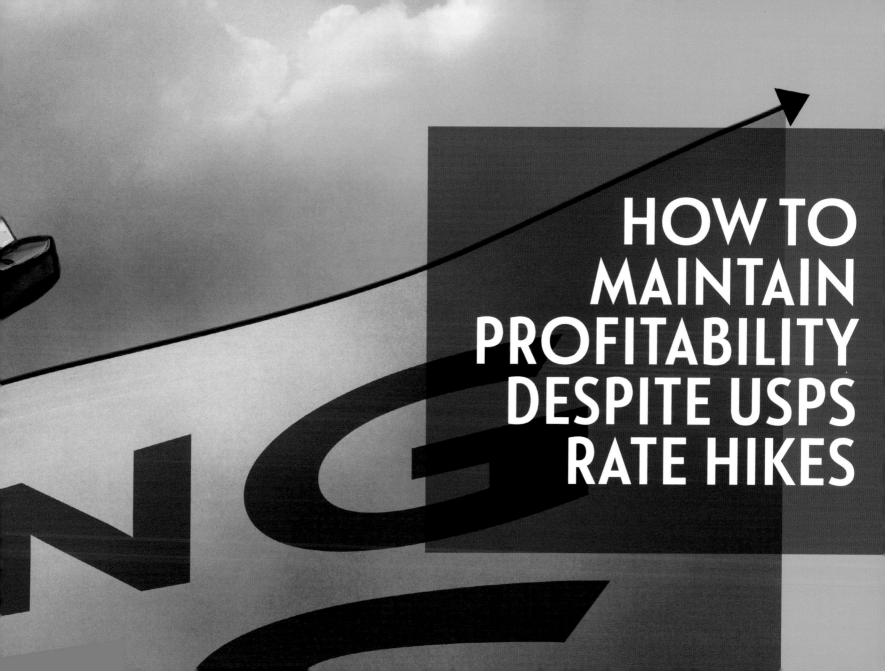

HOW TO MAINTAIN PROFITABILITY DESPITE USPS RATE HIKES

The main goal of every business is to be profitable. You may have other secondary goals, such as providing an amazing customer experience or creating an eco-friendly business. In addition, you may also have visionary goals, like changing the face of your niche or bringing a new product to market.

But for any of those goals to be realized, you must accomplish your primary goal of creating and maintaining profitability. Your ability to become and remain profitable determines whether your business will still exist next year. For some business owners, when they think of maintaining or increasing profitability, they focus on revenue.

You've likely done endless research and expended much effort in learning ways to find more customers. You've probably invested just as many resources in trying to increase the average value of each order.

And rightfully so, it's all important.

All too often the hunt for new customers only distracts business owners from a variable that is just as important to their success – and that is managing costs. You may have gone through painstaking negotiations to find the most cost-effective suppliers. And perhaps you've endured many rounds of trial and error in attempts to get the highest ROI on your ad spend. Even if you've done your due diligence in these areas, maintaining and increasing profitability can still be a challenge at times. It doesn't help that some costs like shipping are out of your control. Almost every year there seems to be an increase in shipping rates and this year is no different. In fact, the United States Postal Service announced that it would be increasing rates effective Sunday, January 27, 2019. Unfortunately, the USPS has a government-mandated monopoly for shipping small packages. If you're unhappy with UPS, you can switch to FedEx and vice versa. There is no such alternative to shipping with USPS.

How will this affect your business and what can you do about it?

How will new USPS rates affect shipping costs

The word 'first-class' may evoke associations with desirability, greatness, and the best option. Yet it turns out that the USPS First Class Package Service (an expedited shipping service used mainly by businesses for fulfillment of packages under 1 lb.) may be one of the worst shipping options for many sellers. Many

Almost every year there seems to be an increase in shipping rates and this year is no different

other delivery options will see about a 5% rate increase on average, but the first-class increase will be significant, in some cases over 10%.

Originally, first-class pricing was uniform to be in line with the Postal Service's Universal Service Obligation (USO), a collection of requirements designed to ensure that everyone in the country receives a minimum level of mail service at a reasonable price. Under the 2018 rates, no matter where you were shipping the package to – cost was determined solely by weight. For example, a one-ounce package costs $2.66 to ship regardless of geographic zone. And a 15.999-ounce package, the heaviest package you can send first class, costs $4.94 to ship to anywhere in the country.

Now, under the new rate changes, First Class Package Service shipping will move to zone-based pricing to better align with the cost of service and improve value based on distance. Zone 1 is the area closest to the sender and Zone 9 is the furthest away, such as in cases of shipping coast to coast. The change to zone-based pricing will cause palpable rate increases. To illustrate, shipping a 5-oz package to zone 7 under the new rates will be close to a 20% price increase.

Here are the new 2019 rates.

What does the new rate change mean for sellers?
You might be offering free shipping as an incentive to get customers to order. However, with the new variable shipping costs, it will be challenging to offer free shipping while accurately maintaining your projected profit margins. You can set regional shipping fees, but you can't adjust your price per region, so it's almost impossible to mitigate the cost of free shipping for a package going across the country.

In addition to making free shipping offers unwieldy to manage, the new zone-based pricing puts domestic sellers at a disadvantage to their international competitors.

While the withdrawal of the U.S. from the Universal Postal Union (UPU) took away international sellers' competitive advantage by no longer allowing them the benefit of discounted shipping rates, the new zone-based pricing neutralizes this potential benefit to domestic sellers.

Also, in light of the new zone-based pricing, it's now more advantageous to ship from mul-

First Class Package Service shipping will move to zone-based pricing

tiple warehouses. If your business is on one of the coasts and you need to fulfill an order on the opposite side of the country, it makes sense to have a warehouse closer to your customer to avoid shipping across higher zones. SellerCloud can automate the process of deciding which warehouse to ship from with our after order plugin. We also provide integrations with 3PL systems.

It's also worth noting that even though the new zone-based pricing might change how you do business, there is still a silver lining. Even with the rate increases, the USPS rates are transparent. There aren't any fuel surcharges or hidden fees.

Whether you're using USPS exclusively or together with other mail carriers, it's important to make sure that your shipping calculations are accurate. Many SellerCloud clients import their shipping invoices into the system to ensure that all fees are accurately reflected in the shipping cost, and to make sure their P&L is accurate.

Protecting your profit margins requires vigilance and strategic thinking. But now that you know about the USPS rate hike, you'll be better prepared to mitigate any risk to your bottom

line. One of the best things you can do for your business is to leverage technology to automate some of your processes so you can focus on what's important: protecting and growing your profits.

Contact SellerCloud directly to find out how our tools and expertise can help.

PRICE

SHIPPING RATES

YEARS

HOW TO LEVERAGE FOREIGN CURRENCY VOLATILITY IN YOUR ECOMMERCE BUSINESS

€ $ ¥

For any ecommerce business, it would make sense that the more international markets you're in, the more customers you'll have, the more products you'll sell, and as a result, your business can reap the benefits of its increased bottom line. Or perhaps you're looking to source your products from overseas, thinking it'll save some money, or that you'll find unique items which you can't find locally. However, it's important to keep in mind that whenever you're selling to international customers or buying from manufacturers abroad, you're exposing your business to volatile currency markets. These fluctuations in the currency markets can have a significant impact on the cost and pricing of your goods, and ultimately your company's profits.

Foreign exchange rates can move by as much as 10% over just a few weeks or even days. There are several factors which can cause these fluctuations, such as political events and elections, economic data and forecasts, central bank meetings, commodity prices, and even the weather.

Some of these events leave only a temporary impact, while others can continue to create volatility for months. For instance, in the weeks following UK's Brexit referendum, the pound fell by 10.4% against the Euro, from €1.3017 on June 23, 2016, to €1.1663 on July 6, 2016.

While volatility can undoubtedly affect your ecommerce business, it can be a currency trader's friend. As major currencies often display high price swings, if trades are placed wisely, the high volatility can help with tremendous profit-making opportunities.

Volatile currency markets don't just impact traders and businesses. Anyone can be affected, positively or negatively. That's why when paying overseas invoices or repatriating profits from abroad, you want to make sure you are getting the best exchange rate and not paying enormous transaction fees. You can avoid this hassle by having a bank account for each currency you are dealing with. Otherwise, banks and international marketplaces such as Amazon will charge their own fees and uncompetitive exchange rates for each currency conversion when depositing your funds into your domestic account. With your currency-specific bank accounts, you can choose when to transfer your money back home, based on the timing of when exchange rates are favorable.

While volatility can undoubtedly affect your ecommerce business, it can be a currency trader's friend

Solutions To Currency Rate Fluctuations

When selling on multiple international marketplaces, your accounting can become a nightmare, especially when it comes to currency conversion for pricing, maintaining profit margins, and calculating your profits and losses (P&L). SellerCloud offers the ideal solution for this.

SellerCloud allows online retailers to consolidate their P&L across their orders from all marketplaces. It will record the currency where each order was placed, and as SellerCloud automatically checks exchange rates once a day, it will save the current rate at the time of the order. You can also search orders across multiple currencies based on the home currency, which is USD for American companies. For example, if you want a list of orders that are valued over $200 USD, it will also include orders for the corresponding value in EUR.

To take your accounting one step further, SellerCloud allows you to export orders into QuickBooks using their multi-currency feature. By default, your foreign currency orders will post to QuickBooks in USD using the conversion rate which SellerCloud had automatically saved at the time of purchase, or you can export orders in their native currency.

When you purchase your goods from an overseas manufacturer, you may need to pay for them in their home currency, which can lead to more confusion when trying to determine your cost of goods sold (COGS) and their profitability. Luckily, SellerCloud supports international currency purchase orders (POs) and allows you to control the conversion rate on the PO, based on the rate at the time you paid for the goods.

No matter which marketplace you're selling in, you still need to stay on top of your pricing to remain competitive, while also maintaining your profit margins. Add in fluctuating currency rates, and that can complicate your pricing strategies even more. The good news is that SellerCloud allows you to easily adjust your item prices across all marketplaces. You just add the base currency on your company profile and your prices on the international marketplaces will auto-adjust based on the current exchange rates using a rating API. You can even convert currencies in bulk on multiple selected SKUs at once.

Another bonus of using the SellerCloud

> **Luckily, SellerCloud supports international currency purchase orders (POs)**

system is taking advantage of our partnership with XE, which is the leading foreign exchange provider. Through this partnership, you can accept and deposit payments locally, then exchange whenever the rates are most favorable. You can even lock-in your rate for up to three years, so you can rest easy that your funds won't be manipulated by currency fluctuations.

Whether you are an entrepreneur or a consumer, I'm willing to bet that you have a PayPal account. Did you know that PayPal, unlike most other payment processors, can hold multiple currencies in one account? You can open a balance in any of their supported currencies, make or accept payments in these currencies, convert your balance from one currency to another, and even close out your balance in any currency you choose. Pretty cool, right? Even better is that SellerCloud's integration with PayPal allows you to charge credit cards for orders, refund payments, capture payment details, and send PayPal invoices – all in multiple currencies!

Why Should I Expand Internationally?
There's no doubt that expanding your ecommerce business globally brings both chal-

lenges and opportunities. As the domestic market tightens and becomes more competitive, an increasing number of sellers are expanding abroad. In fact, Shopify's data from The Enterprise Guide to Global Ecommerce anticipates a 246.15% increase in worldwide ecommerce sales, from $1.3 trillion in 2014 to $4.5 trillion in 2021. That's more than a threefold growth in online revenue.

It's not just B2C ecommerce that's seeing a global explosion, but B2B ecommerce sales are seeing even more growth. According to Statista's B2B Ecommerce 2017 Report, B2C ecommerce sales were $2.3 trillion, while B2B ecommerce sales were $7.7 trillion. SellerCloud has expanded its integrations to include a number of foreign marketplaces, including Amazon Canada, Amazon UK, and Walmart Canada, to name a few.

International marketplaces are like the new frontier for ecommerce entrepreneurs. They represent uncharted territory and raise many questions, such as where should you invest first? Which countries present the best market for your products? Who should you partner with for global warehousing and third-party logistics? I should note that many SellerCloud clients use Shipwire for

It's not just B2C ecommerce that's seeing a global explosion, but B2B ecommerce sales are seeing even more growth

worldwide logistics and fulfillment services. SellerCloud's integration with Shipwire
allows your multi-channel orders to be processed and fulfilled, then updated inventory
and order shipping confirmations will sync
back to your SellerCloud system.

If you aren't selling internationally yet,
you, like many other ecommerce businesses, may be experiencing a severe case of
FOMO-fear of missing out. If you are ready
to jump into the global ecommerce pool
and get your feet wet with the prospect of
new revenue streams, just make sure you're
protecting your profits from those volatile
sharks known as foreign currency fluctuations. Get in touch with SellerCloud to see
how our tools can leverage these volatilities
to your advantage.

EURUSD

BTCUSD

LTCBTC

+3,46%

+0,37%

-0,08%

BLOG.SELLERCLOUD.COM